Praise for How to Make Your Credit Sparkle

"I was amazed at how easy it was to get my credit back in shape. Your course changed my life!"

— Cynthia Farooq, Dallas, TX

"I just wanted to let you know that by following the suggestion in your book I raised my credit score 85 points! And, I just got approved for a mortgage for my first house. I'm going to buy a new car, but only *after* the closing — just like you taught us. Thank you so, so much."

— Maria Nunez, Houston, TX

"I was facing foreclosure, and I thought the only way to save my house was to declare bankruptcy. At least that's what the lawyer told me, before taking his $600 fee. Three months later, I lost my house anyway. After reading your material, I learned what I could have done to save my house and my credit. Even if I knew about your book sooner, I probably would have waited for my financial problems to "solve themselves." They don't. Now I know exactly how important your book is, and I recommend it to all my friends."

— Allen Billings, Seattle, WA

"I tried credit counseling to help with the bills — what a *huge* mistake! They actually made my credit *worse,* and didn't do anything I couldn't have done for myself. With your help, I was able to get the collection companies off my back until I was ready to pay the bills. Thanks Ameen!"

— Jeff Wilson, Kansas City, MO

After reading your book, I found a number of the problems that you specifically warned about on my husband's credit report. Instead of spending big money on credit counseling or credit repair services, everyone should make a small investment in your book, and put themselves in the driver's seat. This book offers a sure-fire way to improve your understanding of credit issues *and* your credit score.

— Gina Gerboth, Colorado

I am writing you this letter to tell you how much I enjoyed reading *How To Make Your Credit Sparkle.* I would like to tell you two ways I have put your book to work for me, and how I am influencing others to clean up their credit via your book!

At first I bought the book for my own benefit. I am new to the "Mortgage World" and have learned so much about so many different aspects of this business, including credit, especially how bad my credit is. After reading through your book it was obvious to me that I really needed to let my clients know about this wonderful book! I can't tell you how many I have turned on to this book. Not only have we (my wife and I) started the process of cleaning up our credit, but we're helping clients and potential clients as well.

I have a special place in my heart for the sub prime clients, because I was one. Notice I said WAS! Thanks to your book, I am well on my way to becoming 100% "A" Paper.

Thanks Ameen!

— Justin Wilks, Spokane WA

How To Make Your Credit Sparkle...

And Everything Else You Need To Know About Your Credit

by Ameen Kamadia

Published by Kamrock Publishing LLC, Houston Texas.

www.creditsparkle.com

For information on multiple copy discounts, licensing, or affiliate programs, please contact the publisher at the website listed above.

More information on Ameen Kamadia's award winning newsletter and one-on-one counseling is also available at the website listed above.

ISBN: 978-0-9753756-2-4

Printed in the United States of America

Library of Congress Cataloging-in-Publication data available upon request from the publisher.

Table of Contents

CHAPTER 1

The Credit Industry

Credit Reports

Credit has become a fact of life. Without it, you are penalized; with it, life becomes easier. Everywhere you turn companies are offering to lend you money, but only if you qualify.

Your "credit" is nothing more than a report containing a history of any accounts you have had in the past or have now. It is not, nor can it ever be, completely accurate—even though it is supposed to be. In fact, the government says you have the right to an accurate report.

CREDIT SECRET: The government says you have the right to an accurate credit report.

Theoretically, your credit report represents an accurate history of your payment habits over the last few years. Credit reports are used in a number of financial transactions, and more and more uses for them are thought up all the time. All applications for credit cards, personal loans, or real estate transactions require credit reports. Increasingly, employers, landlords, immigrations, and insurance companies are checking credit reports.

This book has been written to help you avoid the frustrations and confusion most people feel when working with their credit, and to give you the tools to effectively deal with the credit bureaus without being intimidated by them.

I would estimate that 80% of all reports contain inaccurate information. And most of the other 20% of reports that contain no errors have no credit either. So, if you actually have credit, your chances of having one or more errors on your report are much greater than 80%.

CREDIT SECRET: Eighty percent of all credit reports contain inaccurate information.

First off, let's look at the credit industry. Credit bureaus (also called credit reporting agencies) are private companies that maintain records on everyone's credit. They collect, process, then sell this information to whoever 1) has a legitimate reason for needing it and 2) will pay for it. There are hundreds of individual credit bureaus, but you need only concern yourself with the Big 3: TransUnion, Experian (formerly TRW), and Equifax (formerly CBI). These are the three main bureaus in the U.S. Each of them has a file on you, and each bureau's file is probably different.

There are hundreds of local bureaus, all of which are affiliated with at least one of the Big 3. These bureaus collect information on consumers in a particular region of the country. They then pay to store that information on the computers of one of the Big 3 bureaus. In turn, they get paid every time their information is used by the three national bureaus.

Resellers purchase reports from the Big 3 then resell them to local companies. For small companies that need to check credit, it is usually cheaper to get reports from resellers than directly from the Big 3. In order to get reports from the Big 3, the company must have the proper computer equipment and must go through an extensive registration process to become a subscriber. There might also be membership fees in addition to the cost per report. Since resellers pull reports in a higher volume, they get price discounts.

From now on, I will be referring to the Big 3 when I say "credit bureau." If I am talking about any other kind of bureau, I will call them credit reporting agencies.

Please note that all credit bureaus and reporting agencies are private companies regulated by the Federal Trade Commission (FTC). They are not government agencies. They are in business to make money.

CREDIT SECRET: All credit bureaus are in the business to make money.

Credit bureaus are dependent on the information with which they are provided. For an example, let's say you have a Sears® credit card. Unless Sears notifies the credit bureau that you have this card, the card will not show up on your report. Additionally, if Sears only tells Equifax that you have this card, then only your Equifax report will show the card, while your TransUnion and Experian reports will not. This is the main reason the bureaus can, and usually do, have different information in your file. Not all credit grantors bother to give information to all three bureaus. Most collection agencies in particular only report collection accounts to one bureau.

How Your Credit Is Formed and How They Get the Info

Most people do not realize exactly how information about them is gathered. Nowadays, personal information is big business. Privacy is a thing of the past. Parts of your credit history, your medical history, your arrest record, and your driving record are all public record, available to anyone who asks. But your credit report is supposed to be a private matter.

The credit bureaus do not go out and look for information to put on your report. They could care less. Companies come to them to report your payment habits. These companies do this to protect themselves. If you do not pay, often their only recourse is to mess up your credit. And they can only do this if they report the account to the bureaus in the first place.

Your credit report is filed in the bureaus' computers under your Social Security number. Without this number, a company cannot report any information, good or bad, to the bureaus. ***That is why it is extremely important to protect your Social Security number. Do not give it out to anyone unless you have to, especially to someone with whom you might be doing business.***

In order for a company to report information about you to the bureau, they must be a member of that bureau, and this costs a lot of money. Credit card companies spend lots of money every month sending updated information on all their thousands of accounts to the credit bureaus.

A company can be a member of all three bureaus or whichever ones they choose. If you are dealing with a national company, they probably report to all three bureaus. If the company is local, like a credit union, it probably only reports to the bureau that is most dominant in your part of the country.

You do not actually have a credit report until someone reports an account or asks to see your report. At that time, information supplied to the bureau is added to their computers and you have a report. If you have no credit and someone requested your report, the only information they would get would be the information that they themselves typed in. This just created a report for you.

The information a company needs to request your report is full name, Social Security number (SSN), address, and date of birth. If they misspell your name or address while typing the request, that information also becomes part of your report. That is part of the reason so many reports have erroneous information in them. Unless you have a common and easily-spelled name, you are likely to have an AKA ("Also Known As") listed on your report. For example, my last name is Kamadia. On my reports, I have AKA: Kamachia. Someone must have misspelled my name when doing an inquiry and now I have that stuck on my report unless I dispute it.

So basically, once you apply for credit, the creditor will ask for your name, address, SSN, date of birth, and other information. If they check your credit, your report will show an inquiry from this company and the date on which they checked. If they decline your request for credit, nothing happens. If they approve you for credit, they will send the information about the new account to the bureau, so they can add it to your file.

Keep in mind that while only members of the bureau can report to them, just about anybody with a legitimate excuse can check your credit.

The bureaus do not alter the information given to them. They only compile it and make it available. If any account on your report has erroneous information (for example late payments when you were never late), it is because the company extending you credit is reporting this information. The problem lies in the information that your creditor is giving to the bureaus. But by law, the bureaus are required to maintain accurate files, and it is up to them to investigate and fix any information you say is incorrect on your report.

If, on the other hand, a company is not a member of the bureau, they do not have to report your account to the bureaus. This is why the majority of companies that you deal with do not show up on your credit report. Some of the companies that do not report to the bureaus are your electric company, your landlord, your corner video store, your rent-to-own furniture places, and your insurance company. But if you do not pay these companies, they can put your account in collections and turn it over to a collection company. The agency can then report your collection on your report.

If you want to keep your record clean, the first rule is to pay your bills on time. If you cannot, then be aware of which companies have your SSN and pay them first, before you pay the others. Again, without your SSN, companies cannot report you to the bureaus.

CHAPTER 2

Your Personal Report

How to Read Your Credit Report

In this book, we will not specifically go through a specific credit report from any one credit bureau. The bureaus change their report styles frequently and if I only showed you how to read one report, it would not be as beneficial. So instead, we will go over the main portions of all reports.

There are five primary categories of information contained in each type of credit report:

- Personal Information
- Credit History
- Public Records
- Inquiries
- Credit Score

HOT TIP: Each type of credit report contains five primary categories of information.

1. Personal Information

A credit report's personal information section includes your:

- Name
- Current and previous addresses
- Social Security number
- Telephone number
- Date of birth
- Current and previous employers

A credit report does NOT include information regarding:

- Race
- Gender
- Religion
- Sexual orientation
- National origin
- Medical history
- Checking or savings accounts

If you use a nickname or alias and have used this to apply for credit, this name will show up as an AKA. You could also have an AKA if someone checking your credit misspelled your first or last name.

Any information given to the bureaus by someone checking your credit is automatically added to your report, whether it is right or wrong. So you might have incorrect previous addresses and employers listed.

2. Credit History

A credit report's credit history section should include a listing of all the credit accounts you have had in the last ten years. Types of credit accounts include:

- Retail credit cards
- Bank loans
- Finance company loans

- Mortgages
- Bank credit cards
- Student loans

HOT TIP: The bureaus state that most credit is removed from your report after it is ten years old. Bad credit is removed after seven years.

The credit history section shows creditors how well you have kept your financial promises. Each entry in this section includes:

- Account number
- Creditor's name
- Amount borrowed
- Amount owed
- Credit limit
- Dates when the account was opened, updated, or closed
- Timeliness of payments
- Late payments (these are noted as negative activity)
- Account's rating

There are three types of accounts: Revolving, Installment, and Other. Revolving accounts are credit cards. Installment accounts are loans with fixed payments. All other accounts are classified as "Other." Each of your accounts is given a rating from 1–9. So if you have a bank MasterCard, which is a revolving account, with no late payments, the rating would be an R1. Anything other than a 1 rating shows negative information. A 2 rating would be for a couple of payments that were 30 days late. A 3 rating would be for several late payments. A 9 rating is an account in collection.

HOT TIP: Each of your accounts is given a rating from 1–9.

Payment History:

0 = Too new to review
1 = Paid as agreed
2 = 30+ days past due
3 = 60+ days past due
4 = 90+ days past due
5 = 120 days past due or in collection
7 = making regular payments in bankruptcy or consumer credit counseling
9 = collection, charged off

A letter assigned to each account will indicate whose account it is and how you are involved.

A = authorized user
B = on behalf of another person
C = Co-maker/Cosigner
I = Individual
J = Joint
M = Maker
T = Terminated
U = Undesignated

HOT TIP: For security purposes, the account number listed will not be the entire account number.

3. Public Records

A credit report's Public Records section includes:

- Tax liens
- Bankruptcies
- Court judgments (including child support judgments)
- Some collections

Any negative activity in this section reflects poorly on your creditworthiness. Even if an item has been paid in full, the presence of even a one-time occurrence indicates a potential future concern for creditors.

Again, credit bureaus say these items can stay on your credit report for up to ten years, whether or not they are repaid. The exception is tax liens, which could stay listed indefinitely. But there are always ways for your creditors to get the accounts listed again after the ten years are up. The collections accounts in this section are posted by collection companies that have been hired by your creditors when their own collection procedures failed. So technically, the same collection account could be listed in both the Public Record section as well as the Credit History section. Congress has passed a law that limits the damage collection agencies can do. ***According to the law, there is a seven-year limit that a negative item can stay on your credit report, and that seven years start 180 days after the account is reported delinquent by the original creditor.***

4. Inquiries

A credit report's Inquiries section includes a listing of all parties who have requested a copy of your credit report. The Fair Credit Reporting Act (FCRA) protects your right to privacy, and so only inquiries from those entities with a permissible purpose should be granted access to your report.

HOT TIP: The Fair Credit Reporting Act (FCRA) protects your right to privacy.

Inquiries that do not appear on the business (the report lenders get) or consumer (the one you get when you request a copy from the credit bureau) versions of your credit report are promotional inquiries or account management inquiries. Both promotional and account management inquiries are not counted as official inquiries.

Promotional Inquiries

Companies looking for potential customers query the credit bureaus' databases based on a set of parameters. They then receive mailing address information for individuals matching their criteria. These companies are not viewing your report. They just want to give people who meet their parameters a firm offer of credit or insurance. In other words, they want to bombard you with sales material. These inquires do not hurt your credit score.

Account Management Inquiries

Credit grantors who have permission to review the credit reports of their account holders may do so on a periodic basis. These are not counted as official inquiries. For example, your credit card company can occasionally check your credit report to see if they should increase your credit line.

5. Credit Score

Your credit score is a risk-based calculation that gives your credit a number score. This makes it easier for creditors to determine what type of credit you have...the better your credit, the better your score. We talk more about this in detail later on.

Common Questions

How long do they keep my credit information?

Payment in full does not remove your payment history. The length of time information remains on your credit file is shown below:

- Credit Accounts:

  Accounts paid as agreed remain for up to 10 years.

  Accounts not paid as agreed remain for 7 years.
- Collection Accounts:

  Remain for 7 years.

  (The time periods listed above are measured from the

date that is shown in the "date of last activity" field of your credit file, which accompanies the particular credit or collection account.)

- Courthouse Records:

  Remain for 7 years from the date filed, except:
  - Bankruptcy—Chapters 7 & 11 remain for 10 years from the date filed.
  - Bankruptcy—Chapter 13 non-dismissed or non-discharged remain 10 years from the date filed.
  - Unpaid tax liens remain indefinitely.
  - Paid tax liens remain for up to 7 years from the date released.
  - Paid or unpaid judgments remain on file 7 years from the file date.
- New York State Residents Only: Satisfied judgments remain 5 years from the date filed; paid collections remain 5 years from the "date of last activity."
- California State Residents Only: All tax liens remain 7 years from the date filed.

CREDIT SECRET: Payment in full does not remove your payment history.

What is Credit Scoring?

Credit scoring is one issue that has caused a lot of confusion for the general public. A credit score is a mathematically calculated number that each consumer is given based on several factors.

In the investment industry, companies that sell bonds are rated by investment services according to how risky those bonds are. For example, a bond rated AAA is much safer than a bond rated BBB.

Your credit history is also rated. Instead of getting letter grades, consumers are given number grades. The higher your number, the better your credit, and the less likely you are going to renege on your obligations (in theory at least).

When you apply for credit, the credit grantor needs to predict whether or not you will pay them back. Scoring helps with this process. Notice that everything on your report is past history. There is no way for a credit grantor to know what your financial situation will be tomorrow. Credit scoring says the best way to predict future behavior is to analyze past behavior.

Not only is your past credit history used as a prediction gauge, but your data is compared to the data compiled by the grantor on other customers. The more your data resembles the data of good paying customers, the higher your score and the greater the chance of being accepted for credit.

Credit applications used to be handled by people. At some small lenders, your application might still be reviewed by a person. But more and more companies are using computers and mathematical equations to approve or reject credit applications. Not only is it cheaper for the company, but it also protects the company from being sued by someone charging discrimination. Computers do not care if you are a minority, have a handicap, or are a woman. Your score is computed based solely on past history.

There are several factors taken into consideration when your score is computed. A detailed list is given in Chapter 8. The general industry standards on creditworthiness can be examined by looking at the 4 Cs: Credit, Capacity or Cash Flow, Collateral, and Character.

CREDIT SECRET: The general industry standards on creditworthiness can be examined by looking at the 4 Cs of credit.

1. Credit

The credit report plays a substantial role in any credit application. In some cases, like applications for credit cards and auto loans, it might be the only thing taken into consideration. The report is supposed to show a history of how the individual has been paying his obligations. By looking at the past, lenders feel that they should get an idea of the future.

2. Capacity/Cash Flow

This element of credit helps determine if the borrower can afford the payments. In the case of a mortgage, this element is judged by debt ratios. Your housing payment is only allowed to total up to a certain percentage of your income. For conforming loans, the ratios are 28/36. Your monthly housing payment cannot exceed 28% of your monthly income, and your total monthly debt payments cannot exceed 36% of your monthly income.

Creditors like to see a high enough income in order to afford more debt. This element is how they determine your credit limit on credit cards.

3. Collateral

This element details the assets you own. What do you have that creditors can take away if you do not pay? The more you have the better, as far as they are concerned. Collateral alone can sometimes get you credit if you have enough of it.

4. Character

This element shows how stable you are. How long you have worked at the same company, lived in the same place, owned or rented a house, been married or single, these are all things considered under this element. Checking and savings accounts are also a plus.

Because of the importance of credit scores, there is an entire chapter devoted to them later on in the book.

What is an Inquiry?

According to the FCRA, you have the right to know who has been accessing your file. The names of the companies that have seen your credit are listed at the bottom and are known as inquires. Inquiries will stay on your report for up to two years. The bureaus are pretty good at deleting all inquires over two years old from reports. On consumer reports, which you obtain directly from the bureaus, the full names of the companies accessing your file will be listed. On business reports, only abbreviations are given. You can also obtain the addresses and phone numbers of the companies listed on your report by asking the bureaus for them. Be sure to ask for this, since most reports have several listings and it will save you the trouble of finding the numbers yourself.

Make sure you are familiar with the companies listed as inquires on your report. If the report was accessed illegally, you need to know about it and rectify the problem. If a reseller has accessed your file, you might not be familiar with the name. If that is the case, however, the name of the company to whom the reseller sold the report and the reason for the report should be listed. You should be familiar with the company ordering the report from the reseller. If you are not, you should investigate further.

HOT TIP: If you are not familiar with the company ordering your report, you should investigate further.

From a consumer's perspective, inquiries are not good. Having too many inquires can severely hurt your credit score. On the other hand, having none won't help you either. When applying for credit, creditors take into consideration the number of inquiries you have had within the last six months. A large number of inquiries translates into your being desperate for credit, which is not a good sign, and may even be cause for denial.

Who is Allowed to See My Credit Report?

Because credit bureaus can be sued by consumers for letting unauthorized companies access their credit files, the bureaus require that all credit checks be completed only after authorization has been given by the consumer. In fact, they periodically perform audits. Since we were a reseller, Equifax audited our company twice in the last two years. They chose a certain month of the year, randomly picked 10–15 individuals for whom we had pulled credit reports and asked for copies of the written authorizations. Since we required written authorizations on all checks, our company had no problems.

HOT TIP: The bureaus require that all credit checks be completed only after authorization has been given by the consumer.

But notice that it is only once a year or so that we were checked. We were not required to show authorizations for all the reports we had pulled that month, and only one of the three bureaus audited us. And how does Equifax know that the signatures we are sending really belong to the individuals? For all they know, I could have signed all the authorizations myself. Even though our company would never knowingly break the law, there are others out there that might not have moral standards as high as yours and mine.

There are so many people out there who have access to credit reports, there is no way for the bureaus to watch over everyone. The point is: Credit fraud happens on a daily basis, and it is extremely easy to obtain a credit report on just about anyone.

HOT TIP: Make sure your credit report has not been accessed without your knowledge.

Usually, when you apply for a loan, a rental application, or fill out other types of applications, there is a line in the fine print saying that by signing the application you authorize them to check your credit. Be on the lookout for this. You don't have to sign if you don't want to.

There are instances where the FCRA says it is not necessary to obtain your permission to access your credit report. Still, in most of these circumstances, you usually will be asked for written or verbal authorization.

These instances include:

1. Credit grading purposes. Your credit can be checked by someone who is considering granting you credit, with whom you already have an account, or who is trying to collect a debt. The credit can be for household, family, or personal uses. For the purposes of collecting a debt, the following can check your credit: an attorney thinking about suing; a private investigator trying to collect on behalf of a client; a creditor who has been awarded a judgment; a child support agency trying to collect delinquent child support; a tax collector who has been awarded a judgment; or anyone trying to collect a bad check. (Note: Even thought the FCRA says you can check the credit of someone who has written you a bad check, good luck finding someone to provide you with that report without written authorization.)
2. Employment purposes. Your present or potential employer can check your credit. But if your report is used to deny you employment or a promotion, the company must provide you with a copy of it along with a statement stating your right to dispute information contained within the report.
3. Insurance purposes. If you apply for a new insurance policy or renew a policy for household, family, or personal purposes, your credit can be checked. The report cannot be checked to

evaluate a claim you have made unless you give permission. Again, it's usually in the fine print and you give your implied permission when you sign the application.

4. Business purposes. If someone has a need for your credit information for a business agreement that has been initiated by you, then your credit can be checked by the party.

The FCRA also gives specific cases when credit reports may **not** be obtained. They cannot be obtained by attorneys for litigation purposes. For example, if a lawyer was thinking of suing you, he could not obtain your credit report just to see if you were worth suing...not that there aren't other ways of finding out if you have any valuable assets (such as real estate, etc). Since credit reports only show liabilities, they would not be helpful in and of themselves anyway.

HOT TIP: The FCRA also gives specific cases when credit reports may not be obtained.

During or after a divorce, your ex-spouse cannot obtain your credit report. Obtaining a credit report for both parties before the divorce is essential in dividing up the liabilities of the couple. (More about this can be found in the divorce chapter.)

Credit reports also cannot be used for the purpose of marketing products or for any type of market research. The bureaus are not allowed, by law, to sell any of the information in your report to outside companies. For example, mortgage companies might be interested in getting the names of people who have more than one mortgage account. While this information would be helpful to the mortgage company, and could be supplied by the bureau, they will not do so. The only exception to this rule is pre-screening.

CREDIT SECRET: The bureaus are not allowed, by law, to sell any of the information in your report to outside companies.

Pre-screening is a method used by lenders who issue credit cards to obtain the names of potential customers. The creditor could ask the bureaus, for example, for a list of names of all people in New Hampshire with at least two credit cards and no history of late payments. The bureaus then use their computers to gather this list and sell it to the creditor. Based on this information, the creditor then mails out offers for pre-approved credit cards.

HOT TIP: Pre-approval checks do not show up as inquiries on your credit report.

Pre-approval checks will show up on the report that you get directly from the bureaus, but they will not show up on a report pulled by a lender. Your credit score will not be affected either.

If you do accept the pre-approval offer by sending in the application, the lender who determined what your credit limit should be will then pull your report. If your circumstances have changed since they did the initial screening, you may still be rejected.

Because of an update to the FCRA, you now have a way to prevent your file from being included in this screening process. Each credit bureau is required to advertise a toll free number, which you can call to be blocked from these searches. Once you call in, the bureau must block your file within five business days. Your file will remain blocked for two years. If you wish to block your file indefinitely, you'll have to fill out a form, which you can obtain, from the bureaus.

To opt out of receiving pre-screened credit card offers, call: 1-888-5-OPTOUT (1-888-567-8688). The three major credit bureaus use the same toll-free number to let consumers choose not to receive pre-screened credit offers.

CREDIT SECRET: If you wish to block your file indefinitely, you'll have to fill out a form.

According to FCRA, "Any person who knowingly and willfully obtains information on a consumer from a consumer reporting agency under false pretenses shall be fined for no more than $5,000 or imprisoned not more than one year or both.

"Any employee of a consumer reporting agency who knowingly and willfully provides information concerning an individual from the agency's files to a person not authorized to receive that information shall be fined not more than $5,000 or imprisoned not more than one year or both."

Credit exports are mostly supplied for legal purposes. Everyone who checks your credit will show up as an inquiry so you can keep track. If a reseller obtains your file, the reseller must state the name of the company obtaining the report and their reasons for doing so. The permissible purposes are listed below:

- Business need
- Consumer disclosure
- Collection
- Credit transaction
- Insurance
- License or other benefit
- Employment purposes
- Tenant screening
- Auto
- Unsecured
- Secured
- Partially secured

- Home improvement
- Installment sales contract
- Charge account
- Real estate (specific type unknown)
- Recreational merchandise
- Educational
- Lease
- Line of credit
- Mobile home
- Credit card
- FHA real estate mortgage
- VA real estate loan
- Conventional real estate loan
- Real estate mortgage with or without collateral
- Debit card

All of this information will show on the Inquiries section of your report. For example, it will say that reseller ABC checked your report on behalf of END USER 123 for the purpose of a credit transaction.

HOT TIP: All of this information will show on the inquiry section of your report.

If you believe that someone has accessed your file illegally, contact both the bureau and the FTC. This is very important since someone might be applying for credit in your name. If they are successful, they could get the credit to buy whatever they want, leaving you with the bad credit on your report when they don't pay the bill.

How Do Inquiries Affect My Credit Score

Inquiries only affect your score negatively. For every inquiry made, your score drops approximately six to eight points. After two years, the inquiry will come off your report and your score will go back up.

HOT TIP: Inquires stay on your report for two years.

For credit scoring purposes, the bureaus only take into account any inquires made within the past 6 months. If you are trying to raise your credit score, stop applying for credit. The more inquiries, the worse your score, unless you cause the inquiry yourself. When you call the credit bureau and ask for your own credit report, that will NOT affect your score.

At other times, like when you apply for a mortgage or try to buy a car, you will have multiple inquiries from everyone you visit. Mortgage companies cannot quote you a rate without knowing your credit score. And car dealerships cannot finance you without your credit score. So often what happens is, someone looking for a mortgage will have three or more inquires from his mortgage broker and perspective lenders. If this person visits more than one mortgage broker, the inquiries multiply faster.

To solve this problem, the FICO score (acronym for Fair, Isaac & Co.) people say that they have made adjustments where all inquiries from either mortgages or vehicle financing only count as one inquiry. So even if you go to 200 different mortgage companies and they all check your credit, your score will only be affected by one of them.

That would be great, if it was true, but it isn't. I know because I have pulled credit reports on people just minutes apart, and the scores are lower. Much lower. Next time you hear anything different, check with the person making the claim if they have ever pulled someone's credit to test this. Chances are very high that they haven't.

CHAPTER 3

Your Rights

Congress enacted the Fair Credit Reporting Act (FCRA) in 1971. Since then, a lot of things have changed. In 1986, Congress passed a bill updating the FCRA to provide consumers with better protection. And in 2004, Congress amended the FCRA again, so that is would not expire as it was supposed to. They also added a few extras, which we will discuss below.

HOT TIP: Congress enacted the Fair Credit Reporting Act (FCRA) in 1971.

The FCRA has established several "rights" that consumers must have when dealing with credit issues.

Credit Right #1: You can see your own report.

This sounds pretty obvious, but it can be a pain just to get a copy of your own credit report. The three bureaus want you to contact them directly if you wish to see your report.

HOT TIP: You have a right to see your own report.

In order to get your report, you must contact each bureau separately. Remember, you have three distinctly different credit reports. Each bureau has its own file on you and you should get all three reports if you want to know exactly what is being reported. The most significant change made in 2004 was that everyone is allowed to get at least one FREE credit report each year. You can contact the bureaus at the addresses listed below:

CBI/Equifax
P.O. Box 740241
Atlanta, GA 30374
1-800-685-1111
www.equifax.com

Experian (previously TRW)
Consumer Assistance Center
P.O. Box 949
Allen, TX 75013
1-800-682-7654 or 1-800-422-4879
www.experian.com

TransUnion
P.O. Box 390
Springfield, PA 19064
1-800-916-8800 or 610-933-1200
www.transunion.com

To order your free report, do not contact the three bureaus separately. They have set up one central website, a toll-free telephone number, and a mailing address through which you can order your free annual report. You need to provide your name, address, Social Security number, and date of birth. If you have moved in the last two years, you may have to provide your previous address.

To order, click on *www.annualcreditreport.com,* call 877-322-8228, or complete the Annual Credit Report Request Form (print it from *www.ftc.gov/credit*) and mail it to: Annual Credit Report Request Service, P.O. Box 105281, Atlanta, GA 30348-5281.

NOTE: If you get an e-mail or see a pop-up ad claiming it's from *www.annualcreditreport.com* or any of the three nationwide consumer reporting companies, do not reply or click on any link in the message—it's probably a scam. Forward any email that claims to be from *www.annualcreditreport.com* or any of three consumer reporting companies to the FTC's database of deceptive spam at *spam@uce.gov.*

If you request your report online at *www.annualcredit report.com,* you should be able to access it immediately. If you order your report by calling 877-322-8228, your report will be processed and mailed to you within 15 days. If you order your report by mail using the Annual Credit Report Request Form, your request will be processed and mailed to you within 15 days of receipt. Whether you order your report online, by phone, or by mail, it may take longer to receive your report if the nationwide consumer reporting company needs more information to verify your identity.

There may be times when the nationwide consumer reporting companies receive an extraordinary volume of requests for credit reports. If that happens, you may be asked to re-submit your request. Or, you may be told that your report will be mailed to you sometime after 15 days from your request. If either of these events occurs, the nationwide consumer reporting companies will let you know.

For additional reports, you must pay for them. In the past, the charges were as follows:

- In Connecticut, you pay $5 for the first report a year and $7.50 for each report after that. In Maine, you pay $2 plus additional charges for photocopying.
- In Maryland, you get one free copy per year and pay $5.25 for each copy after that. Vermont residents get one free report per year and pay $7.50 afterwards.
- In Georgia, you get two free copies per year.
- All other states, you pay $8 per report.
- Some states charge sales tax; some do not.

You can also get your report free if you've been denied credit. If you have been turned down, the company turning you down must notify you in writing that you were denied and inform you from which bureau they got their information. You can then obtain a free report from that bureau only. Simply mail your request for a free report with a copy of the rejection letter.

CREDIT SECRET: You can get a free copy of your credit report if you've recently been denied credit.

You can also get a free report if:

- You are unemployed and will apply for work within 60 days
- You are on welfare
- You believe you have been a victim of credit fraud
- You have been told by a collection agency affiliated with the credit bureau that they will or have put something on your file.

Credit Right # 2: Your file should be accurate and complete.

Again this should be obvious, but it wasn't so before the FCRA was passed. There have been, and continue to be, many lawsuits filed against the bureaus by consumers as a result of inaccurate information contained in credit files.

How accurate your file needs to be is still unclear. Credit files will never be 100% perfect. There will always be mistakes. But once the mistakes are identified, they should be fixed right away. And that leads up to ...

Credit Right #3: The credit bureaus must fix their mistakes.

If you find erroneous information on your report, the credit bureau must investigate the matter and remove the information if you are right. If they cannot verify the information, they also must remove it from your file.

HOT TIP: The credit bureaus must fix their mistakes.

Currently, the bureaus have 30 days to investigate disputes. If they cannot verify the disputed information within 30 days, they must delete it. If during the investigation you offer additional information, they have another 15 days to work with it. If you do not hear anything in 30 days, do not assume everything is OK. Contact the bureau again, making sure to include a copy of your last letter.

Once something is deleted from your report, it is still possible that it will show up again. If the creditor verifies the information after 30 days, the bureau can then put it back on your file. The bureau must send you a letter within 5 business days, stating that the information is back on your report. They must also include the contact information for the creditor who verified it.

Under the updated FCRA, no one can report information to the bureaus that they "know or consciously avoid knowing" is inaccurate. That means that unless a creditor can provide serious proof that something is accurate, they cannot report it to the bureaus.

CREDIT SECRET: They do this anyway. Mistakes happen.

This new change in the law is more helpful in preventing unscrupulous creditors from placing derogatory information on your report just to hurt you.

Credit Right # 4: Your story.

This right allows you, as a consumer, to add a consumer statement to your file, in which you can say anything you want. The bureaus force you to keep it to 100 words maximum. If you have trouble determining what you want to say, the bureaus must help you word your statement.

Credit Right #5: Very old data should not hurt you.

This part of the law limits the amount of time information can stay on your report. Usually, all accounts except bankruptcies drop off your report after seven years of the last activity. Good credit can stay on indefinitely but the bureaus usually drop closed accounts.

CREDIT SECRET: The bureaus usually drop closed accounts from your credit report after 7 years.

Credit Right # 6: You should be able to understand your report.

Credit reports have become much easier to read and understand. Later in this chapter, we will discuss the various codes bureaus use to distinguish accounts.

If there is something on your report you do not understand, the law says the bureau must explain it to you. The bureaus must maintain free hotlines for consumers with questions. Also, if there is a creditor on your report that you do not recognize or need contact information for, the bureaus must provide you with that information.

Before the FCRA and until the 1990s, credit reports were super confusing and only trained people could decipher them. The bureaus did this on purpose to maintain their secrecy. But since then, they have become more consumer-friendly and continue to make their reports easier to understand for the common person.

Credit Right #7: You should know who has seen your report

Under the Inquiries section of your report, it lists any company that has checked your credit in the past two years. The full name of the company must be provided. Phone numbers and addresses are usually given at the end of the report.

Credit Right # 8: Only people whom you allow to see your report can do so.

The section on Inquiries in this book goes into detail on who can and cannot check your credit. But be warned, even without your written authorization, people can check your credit if they have sufficient reason.

Credit Right # 9: You can sue the bureaus.

If the bureaus willfully violate the FCRA and you can prove it, you can win in court against the bureaus. You should talk to an attorney if you have legitimate proof that information on your report is erroneous and the bureaus will still not remove it. You can sue for either willful noncompliance or negligent noncompliance.

Identity Theft and Your Rights

Identity theft has become an epidemic. It is so ridiculously easy to steal someone's information and get credit in their name that Congress has finally stepped in to help people. In 2003 Congress passed the Fair and Accurate Transactions Act (FACTA) that gives us more rights and ways to deal with identity theft. According to a summation by Consumers Union, the law includes the following provisions:

- If a fraud alert is on a consumer's credit report, lenders will be required to phone the consumer or take other "reasonable steps" to verify the applicant's identity before issuing credit or raising a credit limit. The alert must be included with any credit report or score sold to lenders.
- Any consumer will be able to put a 90-day fraud alert on his or her credit file. The alert can be extended for seven years if the consumer provides an identity theft report, such as the ID theft affidavit provided by the Federal Trade Commission, as long as the report is filed with the local police. Those who file for extended alerts are automatically kept off the marketing lists that bureaus sell to marketers.
- When a consumer files a request for a fraud alert with one bureau, that bureau is required to contact the others.
- Credit bureaus are required to stop reporting accounts or information that a consumer identifies as fraudulent, if the consumer provides an identity theft report. This practice is called trade line blocking.

- After a bureau informs a creditor that a block is in effect, the creditor must have "reasonable" procedures to keep it from reporting the information again to the bureaus.
- When an account has been blocked, the creditor cannot sell or transfer the debt to a collection agency. If the debt is already in collections, the collection agency will be required to notify the creditor that the debt might be fraudulent and to provide the consumer a list of collection rights. But only if the consumer asks for it.
- Businesses where a thief has opened accounts will be required to help the victim produce records that the victim might need to clear their name.
- Credit card machines are required to hide the account numbers on receipts. And consumers can ask that their Social Security number be hidden on the consumer reports that they request.

Please note that all these new rights will be implemented slowly. Some are not required to go into effect until 2007.

The Top Reasons Why Your Report is Incorrect

Just about every report has some errors on it. Some are not as important as others. If some of your accounts are not updated to the current month, it is not as big of a deal as if there is some erroneous negative information. Let's discuss the three major disputes people have with their reports, what to do about them and how to avoid them in the future.

Unknown accounts on your report

If these accounts are not yours, it could be because:

- They belong to someone with the same or similar name.
- They belong to someone living at your address.

- The creditor entered your SSN on the account instead of the real account holder's SSN.
- Someone is stealing your identity.
- They belong to an ex-spouse, a child or a parent.

What to do:

Call the creditor reporting the account right away. Find out who opened it and when they did so. If they admit it is not your account, get them to fax you something in writing that says so. This will make it easier to dispute it from your credit report. If they will not talk to you at all, dispute the account with the bureaus.

CREDIT SECRET: If your credit report is incorrect, call the creditor reporting the account right away.

How to avoid this problem:

- If you have a common name, use your middle name or at least a middle initial.
- Write clearly and legibly on all credit applications.
- Do not name your child after yourself. This will cause problems for both of you.
- Use a nickname when applying for credit. Robert could become Ricky.

If there are inaccurate late payments on your account, then it could be because:

- The creditor's computers are incorrect.
- You are not mailing your payments on time.
- The payment could have been posted to another account.

What to do:

It's a good practice to keep all your statements for about two years. This is for tax purposes as well as personal reasons. If you have late payments listed, you can refer back to the statements you have. If on the following month's statement you were not charged a late fee, or it shows your payment was received, then you have proof that you were never late.

How to avoid this problem:

- Check your statements every month to make sure your payments are being posted and that you recognize all the charges.
- Mail your payments at least five days before the due date printed on your statement.
- If you don't have enough money even for the minimum payment, send in something. If they see you are making an effort, you might just get away with a late fee.
- Staple your check to the part of the statement that you return to the creditor. They always ask that people do not do this so that they don't have to waste their time taking out the staples. However, this ensures that your check doesn't get "lost."
- Use the envelope that comes with the statement to mail your payment. This speeds up the processing of your payment.
- Write your account number on your check. Never send cash. You can't trace cash if they say they never received it.

HOT TIP: Mail your payments at least five days before the due date.

Medical collections

Been to a doctor or hospital lately? If so, you have a great chance of having a medical collection. Medical collections have become the number one cause of credit errors today. The problem is so bad that many lenders, especially mortgage companies, just ignore them. Even so, they still affect your score. A collection could drop your score between 20–50 points.

You would think that the insurance company would take care of the bill. In the event that they don't, or if they take too long, you get put into collections until the bill is paid. It's not fair but there isn't much you can do about it.

CREDIT SECRET: Medical collections have become the #1 cause of credit errors today.

PERSONAL STORY: While lifting a bucket of water at one of my businesses, I hurt my back. I figured if I lay down the pain would go away in a few minutes. Big mistake. When I tried to get up, I couldn't. The pain was just too intense. I couldn't even sit up, so I called for help. My employees tried to lift me and take me to the car, but I couldn't move. As a result, we had to call an ambulance.

The paramedics took me to the emergency room of the nearest hospital. I was admitted and put into a room, still unable to even sit up on the gurney they had brought me in on. After two hours, someone decided to take me to get an x-ray. After another three hours, the doctor showed up and said that the x-ray was negative and that it must be a muscle sprain. After another hour, they gave me an injection of some painkiller. Thirty minutes later, they forced me into a wheelchair (the painkiller was working), and my dad took me home. It took six hours to get one injection and one x-ray! Perhaps you can tell that I am still angry about the whole thing, but it gets even worse.

Three weeks later I got a bill from the ambulance company for $400. I paid that right away, yet four months later I get a call at home from the hospital saying I need to pay them. For some reason they didn't have my address. So I paid them over the phone with my credit card—$469. Then a couple months later, I'm checking my credit report when I see one bureau is reporting a collection of $303, listing it from the hospital. I call them up and they say it must be from the doctor.

So I paid the ambulance and the hospital. Now I have to pay the damn doctor that works for the hospital...the doctor who didn't even spend five minutes with me? That's insane. Unless I'm dying I'm never going back to that house of thieves.

Anyway, I called the collection agency representing the doctor. After yelling at them for not sending me the bill, I informed them they couldn't put anything on my report without giving me a chance to pay it first. I informed them they would not get any money from me unless they removed the collections from my report. They faxed me a letter saying they would remove the collection if they got my payment. I sent them the money and my credit is now clean again.

What to do:

If your insurance was supposed to cover the medical expenses, dispute the collection with the credit bureau and bother your insurance company until they pay off the account.

How to avoid this problem:

- Pray it doesn't happen to you.
- Make sure the hospital has all your current information including address and phone number.
- If your insurance is supposed to pay the hospital, call the hospital and find out if they have been paid. If not, bother the insurance company until they do.

- If you have a dispute with the insurance company over what they are supposed to pay, get yourself a medical billing advocate. They charge between $30 and $150 an hour. Remember, fixing the problem before it is on your credit report is always better. Check out *www.claims.org* and *www.billadvocates.com*.

HOT TIP: If your insurance company was supposed to cover the medical expenses, bother them until they pay off the account.

How to Keep Your Credit Clean

1. Pay your bills on time.

Your payment is late if you miss a payment for 30 days. That means you will not be reported late unless you skip a payment. If the due date is on the 17th of the month, and they do not get your payment by that date, you will be charged a late fee. However, it will not be reported to the credit bureau unless your payment is not received or if it is received after the next month's statement is sent out.

Not all of your creditors report their information to the bureaus, so if your money is short, pay the ones who report first. In order of importance, you should pay your mortgage, car payment, credit cards, store cars, gas cards, student loans and child support.

Generally, your rent, your utilities, your personal loans, your rent-to-own arrangements and your cell phone payments are not reported to the bureaus unless you do not pay them at all and they put your account in collections.

HOT TIP: To keep your credit clean, pay your bills on time.

2. Close accounts you are not using.

The more accounts you have, the greater the chance that things will get messed up. If your account has a high balance and several late payments, it looks good if you close the account. The account will be labeled as "closed by consumer." Creditors like this since it shows that you are interested in not running up more debt and want to get your accounts under control.

3. Pay down your debts as soon as possible.

If you are serious about fixing your credit and your financial situation, then pay down your debt. Reducing your balances is probably the second best way to increase your credit score. Talk to any collection companies that are listed on your report and negotiate with them to get your account paid off. You should be able to get the amounts reduced by about half. Do not let them push you around. And, in any deal you make with them, you should try to get them to take the collection off your report. Make sure you get everything in writing before you send them any money.

4. Do not apply for new credit.

Inquiries hurt your score. Every inquiry can lower your score 5–10 points each. If you already have a financial situation, you do not need to dig the hole any deeper. You need to condense your credit, not expand it.

CREDIT SECRET: Don't dig your hole any deeper by applying for new credit cards.

5. Dispute and remove all untrue derogatory information on your report.

If a negative account is from a company that is out of business, such as a bank that has been bought by another bank, dispute it. The paperwork will most likely not be available. If the negative account is over five years old, dispute it. Once again the chances are good that the account will be removed.

6. Add good accounts that are not reported.

If you have been granted credit from local retailers and it is not on your report, tell the bureau to add it. Each bureau has its own way of doing this, but you only need to contact one of them. They are supposed to share all information.

7. Consolidate as much debt as possible.

By consolidating you are taking your balances from two or more sources and putting them all on one account. This pays off your other accounts and should lower the interest rate as well. This will help you because now you have accounts which are not maxed out (that shows you are not in a money crisis). The amount you have borrowed compared to the amount you can borrow is a major factor in determining your credit score. The higher your credit limits are, and the lower your balances are, the better.

CHAPTER 4

Fixing Your Report

Disputing Information on Your Credit Reports

The following chapter will outline generic instructions on how to go about successfully disputing information on your credit report. When dealing with credit bureaus you need to remember that you are dealing with large bureaucracies who are not really interested in helping the individual consumer.

Experian makes it a point to inform resellers of its reports that all of the files are Experian property. Even though it is information about you and me, we do not own our own files! These bureaucracies take their sweet time in doing anything. They do what they are required to do by law and not much more. If you have a legitimate dispute in which your credit contains erroneous information, the bureaus will be glad to help you remove it. That will make their files more reliable and, more importantly for them, will keep you from suing them. The bureaus spend millions of dollars every year defending themselves in court from lawsuits filed by consumers. They want to limit these suits as much as possible.

On the other hand, if the bureau suspects that you are working with a credit repair company or trying to fix your credit on your own, they might just toss your initial disputes in the trash. If this happens you will need to get "tough" and you'll learn how to do that in the next few pages.

CREDIT SECRET: If a bureau suspects that you are working with a credit repair company or trying to fix your credit on your own, they might just toss your initial disputes in the trash.

The first thing you need to do is to obtain your credit report from all three bureaus. When dealing with the bureaus, you will need to be very organized and document every correspondence, leaving a nice detailed paper trail. It is best to keep a separate file for each credit bureau and each creditor you will be dealing with. Keep copies of every letter mailed to them as well as everything received from them. Note the date on the top of their correspondence or when it was received. Keep your files in chronological order. Also, any time you speak with someone on the phone, make sure to take notes on what was said, the full name of the person you spoke to, his position, the date and time of the call and what was agreed to. It is also a good idea to get the name and direct phone number of the person's superior.

CREDIT SECRET: When dealing with the bureaus, you need to leave a detailed paper trail.

Once you start receiving your reports, you will need to understand them thoroughly. You should also know how to identify any information that needs to be disputed. How to read and understand reports has already been covered earlier in this book. Some common errors on reports are:

- The information on your credit report belongs to someone else, either someone of a similar name or address. This is called file co-mingling.
- Your name is misspelled; your address, birth date, or SSN is wrong.
- Your former spouse appears on your accounts.
- Unauthorized inquires are listed on your report.
- Account information is inaccurate or incomplete.
- Accounts showing late payments may not be updated to show you are current. Balances on your accounts are wrong if the account has not been updated.
- Closed accounts could still be showing as open. Common errors of this type involve mortgages. Mortgages are usually sold to secondary lenders soon after you take out the mortgage. Once it is sold, the secondary lender now shows up on your report with the mortgage amount outstanding. But in many cases, the original lender's account still shows a balance rather than zero. Thus, your report shows you now have two mortgages with the same or similar balances.

Once you receive your reports, make one or two copies of them to work with. You will need to send the original back with your dispute. On one copy of your report, mark or highlight all negative items contained in it. On the other copy, mark all items that are inaccurate. These could be accounts that do not belong to you, old accounts that have not been updated, duplications of the same account, or anything similar.

HOT TIP: All correspondence with the bureaus should be sent certified mail, return receipt requested.

All correspondence with the bureaus should be sent certified mail, return receipt requested. This will cost a little more and will require you to physically go to the post office, but it is an essential part of your paper trail. You will have proof that you sent your dispute and the exact date it was received by the bureau. Staple the return receipts to the copies of the letter sent and keep them in your files.

Each dispute will be handled by a person. These individuals are trained to sniff out "frivolous disputes." Since the law is still vague about what a "frivolous dispute" is, these individuals must have a good reason not to throw your dispute away. If they suspect any wrongdoing on your part, they will do exactly that. The two most important items you will need to rebuild your credit will be time and patience. Be prepared to write several letters to the bureaus. Don't let your letters sound like form letters or they most probably will be ignored.

HOT TIP: The two most important items you will need to rebuild your credit will be time and patience.

Once you have identified all the accounts you need to dispute, it is time to develop your dispute letter. Use the following rules to guide you.

The Rules for Disputing Your Credit Report

1. Never lie about anything that you send to the credit bureaus or on a credit application. It is now a crime to make untrue or misleading statements on disputes and applications. It is your right to dispute any information for *which you have reason to believe* is

untrue, inaccurate, or obsolete. Even true items on your report can be disputed if you have reason to believe that they may not be verifiable. If you lie, and are found out, you could be held responsible for committing credit fraud.

2. Clearly state the account you are disputing and what exactly about the account you are disputing. If you don't clearly identify what you think is incorrect, the dispute will be returned to you. The bureaus cannot, and will not, begin an investigation unless they know whether you are disputing the account being on your report or if you are disputing a certain part of the account such as the late payments or the balance.

HOT TIP: The bureaus will not begin an investigation unless they know what you are disputing.

If the account is not yours, label it as "not my account" on the dispute letter. After the investigation, if the bureau finds that it really isn't your account, it will be completely removed from your report. If you are disputing a particular aspect of the account, after the verification, the information being disputed will be corrected and the rest will be left unchanged.

3. Tell the bureau what you would like them to do with the disputed credit information. I know this sounds like common sense, but it helps in processing your dispute faster.
4. Do not waste your time disputing information in a negative account. Negative accounts would be collections, charge offs, public records, repossessions or foreclosures. The fact that the account is negative hurts you several times more than any specific information contained within the account. These accounts should be disputed and taken off the report entirely or not disputed at all. The only exception is if you have paid off the amount and it is still showing a balance.

5. Add your own story. Lend a human touch to your disputes. Computers cannot process disputes; people still need to do that. The more touching and personal your story is, the more likely the person checking into your dispute will want to help you. Add sentences to your letter that explain your personal situation. You might want to tell them a little about yourself. The bureaus receive millions of disputes every year. If you can make yours stand out, you might have a better chance of getting faster service.

CREDIT SECRET: Computers cannot process disputes; people still need to do that.

6. Don't use legal language. You don't want your letter to sound as if it is coming from an attorney or a credit repair company. Quoting a statute of law or reminding the bureau your rights might lead the checker to assume you are attempting credit repair. I'd be willing to bet that the checkers at the bureaus have competitions to see which among them can spot the most credit repair disputes.
7. Use polite language in your first two or three disputes. The first ones will be the easiest to fix. As you send in more and more, it will successively become harder to get them to start an investigation. Use stronger language with each dispute. Different techniques involve threatening to write the FTC, your state attorney general, the Better Business Bureau, or vowing to hire an attorney. It would be wise not to threaten a lawsuit unless you intend to go through with it or unless you are down to your last straw.

HOT TIP: Use stronger language with each dispute.

8. Do not send several disputes one right after another. This will definitely not work. All your disputes will be out in the frivolous dispute box, also known as the garbage can. A good timetable is to send a dispute 60–90 days after you sent in the last one.
9. Use the bureaus against each other. If one bureau does not show negative information on an account, make sure you tell the others. Use every piece of information available on your reports in your disputes.
10. Mail all your disputes via certified mail, return receipt requested.
11. Send original disputes every time. Creating your disputes on your computer is best. You'll have back ups as well as be able to make corrections to it for follow-up letters.
12. Draft your own dispute letters. Do not use the dispute forms sent to you with your credit report. These forms can put words in your mouth and may even cause you to lie, which is against the law.
13. Include a copy of your driver's license and Social Security card. If you don't, the bureaus will simply mail back your dispute. They will not start working on it until you submit "proof" of who you are.

Plan of Action:

1. Order your credit report from all three bureaus.
2. Do not wait to receive all three. Start as soon as you receive the first one.
3. Mark all incorrect information to be disputed.
4. Draft your first dispute letter, adding your personal touch. Dispute negative information or accounts that do not belong to you first. If there are other problems, such as incorrect SSN or

address, leave this for later since they are easier to get changed. Dispute one item at a time and only one per letter.

5. Mail the dispute via certified mail, return receipt requested. Make sure to include all personal information such as name, address, SSN and date of birth.
6. After receiving your response, send a follow-up letter immediately if necessary. Otherwise, wait 30–60 days from the date you sent the last one before sending your next one.
7. Repeat for each item to be disputed.

If all three bureaus show the same erroneous information, you can do one of three things:

1. Dispute the item with only the first bureau. Wait until they take it off then dispute it with the other two. Once the creditor who reported the false information notices that the information is wrong, they should tell the other two bureaus themselves. In any event, dispute it with the other two bureaus just to be safe.
2. Dispute it with all three bureaus at the same time. Depending on the creditor's system, this could take a while longer since all three parties will be requesting the same information.
3. Dispute it with the creditor. If you are a current customer of the creditor, they should be happy to investigate for you while you are on the phone. If they agree and say they will tell the bureaus to remove the information, make sure you tell them to send you a copy of all of letters they send to the three bureaus.

HOT TIP: You can do one of three things if all three credit bureaus show the same erroneous information.

Restoring your credit is not an easy process. In an ideal situation, the credit bureau will investigate, agree with you that they are wrong and delete any and all negative information from your report. That's not the way it always happens, however. You will probably receive rejections or stall tactics more often than you get positive responses. After sending off your dispute to the bureaus, you will get one of eight responses from them.

They are:

1. You will receive a new credit report with the results of the investigation.
2. You will receive a letter stating that your dispute has been forwarded to the appropriate credit bureau.
3. You will receive a letter stating that the bureau has begun the investigation.
4. You will receive a rejection letter because the bureau thinks you are attempting credit repair.
5. You will receive a rejection letter because the dispute is "frivolous or irrelevant."
6. You will receive a rejection letter because of the timing of your dispute.
7. You will receive a letter ASKING for more information.
8. You will receive no response whatsoever from the bureau.

HOT TIP: You will get one of eight responses regarding your dispute with the credit bureaus.

Equifax and TransUnion provide a list of disputed items and whether or not the items were changed, deleted, or verified as accurate. Experian only provides a list of the disputed items. Once your dispute has been investigated, you will see one of four results:

1. The account you stated as not belonging to you was incorrect or unverifiable and was deleted from your report.
2. The item you disputed was verified as accurate and there was no change.

3. The item you disputed was inaccurate or unverifiable so the account is now free of the disputed item.
4. An item that was previously deleted is now back on your report.

HOT TIP: Once your dispute has been investigated, you will see one of four results.

If the item you disputed was not changed, you have the right to dispute it again. It is not recommended that you dispute it right away, unless this is the only item left to correct.

Items that were previously deleted can reappear on reports. If an item is disputed and the creditor does not respond to the bureau's investigation, the bureau has no choice but to remove the item. But if the creditor verifies the item after the item has been deleted, the bureau can put it back on your report. This type of item would then need to be redisputed.

Unverifiable accounts are those for which the creditor no longer has records of the account. This could happen if the creditor has gone out of business, is bought out by another firm, changed computer systems, or if the account is very old.

CREDIT SECRET: A good way to determine if an account will be unverifiable is to call the company yourself and ask for the account's status.

A good way to determine if an account will be unverifiable is to call the company yourself and ask for the account's status. If the customer service representative tells you there is no record of the account in the computer, chances are excellent that the bureau will not be able to verify any information being disputed on this account.

Companies also purge their computers of all closed files after a certain time period, especially if the account was written off. If the account is still in the system, ask the customer service representative when it will be purged.

The more you dispute your credit report, the more difficult it is to have items changed and removed. That's when it's time to get nasty. The bureaus are private businesses. And, like all business, they are there to make a profit. The bureaus' biggest fears are an increase in regulation by the government and additional lawsuits.

CREDIT SECRET: Like any business, credit bureaus are there to make a profit.

How would you react if someone approached you and told you that they had contacted an attorney and were considering filing a lawsuit against you? Most people would be alarmed. Well, the credit bureaus react the same way. Even though they are afraid of lawsuits, they still get sued everyday. They pay hundreds of thousands in claims to citizens whose rights they have violated. They pay even more in attorneys' fees. Anyone can sue the bureaus every time they violate the Fair Credit Reporting Act. Realistically though, the consumers who have the greatest chance of winning their suits are those with negative information on their reports, which is not theirs, and which was not removed by the bureaus.

Threatening a lawsuit should not be overused. Use stronger and stronger language with each dispute. If you don't have to use threats, don't. But don't be intimidated by the bureaus either.

HOT TIP: Threatening a lawsuit should not be overused.

Legislation for stronger credit reporting laws can be enacted by Congress. That's why it works when you write in your dispute that: "if this dispute is not investigated properly I will be forced to write to all my state's Representatives and Senators about it." Sending copies of letters written with your disputes is another trick. The state of Colorado recently passed a law requiring that bureaus provide better service to all residents of Colorado. This pushed up costs and hit the bureaus where it hurts the most—in the pocketbook. You can be sure they didn't like it. They even mentioned that they might stop operating in the state completely. But instead, it now costs more for resellers to obtain reports for Colorado residents. The bureaus just passed on the additional cost to the consumers.

Your third leverage point is the Federal Trade Commission (FTC). The FTC is the government agency responsible for regulating the bureaus and for monitoring their activities. The credit bureaus are always a top source of consumer complaints on record at the FTC. Your single complaint will not make much of a difference to the bureaus, but they would rather you didn't make it.

The FTC can be reached at:

FEDERAL TRADE COMMISSION
Pennsylvania Ave. and Sixth St. NW
Washington, DC 20580
http://www.ftc.gov

Submitting a 100-Word Explanation

As previously noted, it is your right to add a statement to your report—limited to 100 words. This statement is used to explain negative marks on your report. The theory is that creators will see this explanation, will give you the benefit of the doubt and will still extend credit to you. Common explanations include purses or wallets being stolen, being victims of fraud, and dealing with sickness or unemployment.

Just because you add an explanation, do not assume creditors will automatically forgive your negative marks. In fact, most creditors don't even look at them. Loans and credit cards are approved or rejected by computers and the computers cannot read your statement. The credit report format that creditors receive is different from the format consumers receive. In the creditor format, the statement does not usually align properly and hard is to read. Adding a statement is pretty much a waste of your time.

CREDIT SECRET: Most creditors don't even look at the explanations you add to your report.

Dealing with Creditors

Instead of disputing an item with the credit bureaus, sometimes it is easier and faster to deal with the offending creditor, especially if the erroneous information is being reported to more than one bureau.

If the creditor agrees that it was their mistake, get something in writing saying so and have them contact the three bureaus to correct the mistake. It should be erased within one to two months.

CREDIT SECRET: Sometimes it is easier and faster to just deal with the offending creditor.

PERSONAL STORY: I used to have a recurring bill charged to my Chase MasterCard. It was for AT&T WorldNet Internet access and would automatically be charged to my card every month. I wanted to cancel this account and tried calling AT&T. They had a separate division for calls from people wanting to cancel. I guess no one works in that division because no one ever picked up the phone. I tried calling twice and was on hold for more than half an hour both times. So, I called Chase directly. For some reason, the customer service representative told me he could not stop the charges, so I told him to cancel my account and transfer my balance to another, new account. This would cause AT&T to not be able to get any money and they would cancel the account themselves. The rep did this right away and I got the new card with the new account number in a few days.

But the balance on the old account was not zeroed out right away. Chase put a late payment on the old account. Instead of disputing with the bureaus, I called Chase and they verified that it should not have happened. They then faxed me a letter saying it was their mistake and they notified the bureaus to remove the late payment.

A few months later, the late payment was back. So I still had to dispute the late charge with the bureaus, but all I had to do was mail them a copy of the fax and I was done.

Negotiating with Creditors

Negotiating with creditors works when you want them to remove negative information they are reporting, even if it is accurate. If you have an account with a creditor and you owe them money, they are likely to work with you to keep your business. If on the other hand the account is closed, they might still negotiate with you if you still have a balance. If the account is paid off, they have no incentive to negotiate with you. If you have some money and can afford a payment to pay off the account, it might be best for you to do so, if, and only if, they remove the negative remarks from that account or remove it entirely. Your goal is to give them what they want—money—in order to clear your credit.

HOT TIP: Your goal is to give the creditor what they want in order to clear your credit.

When dealing with creditors, negotiate with the one that is reporting the negative information. Only they can make changes to the account on your report. For example, say a collection company calls you about a car loan. If the car loan account listed under the original lender has several late payments, the collection company cannot take those off. Only the original lender can remove those negative notations from your report.

And don't believe them if they say they cannot change anything in your credit file. If they report it, they can change it. If they say they can't, ask for a supervisor. They would rather have their money than give you bad credit.

HOT TIP: So far we have been talking about negotiating unsecured debts.

Not only should you try to get the negative remarks deleted, you should also try to pay them less than you owe them. The size and age of the debt determines if you can get the amount of the debt reduced. When negotiating, tell your creditor what you want and what you will give. Be firm. If they do not give you what you want, tell them "no deal." You have the upper hand. They are more desperate than you should be.

If you want to play hardball, tell them you are considering bankruptcy. Do not say that you are already in or are filing bankruptcy; just say you are thinking about it. If you do go through with such action, they will get nothing. You can also try this tactic: Say you only have a certain amount of money and several creditors. Whoever accepts your offer first will get the money. Good luck.

Dealing with Collection Companies

According to the Fair Debt Collection Practices Act, you have different rights when dealing with collections agencies. For example:

You have the right to have a collection "validated." What this mean is that the collection agency must provide proof that the debt is yours and that they have the right to collect it. And until they provide you with this evidence, they must stop all efforts to collect from you. If they cannot validate, they must remove the account from your reports.

In order to validate, the agency must present documentation—obtained from the original creditor—that proves you owe the money. Most of the time, collection agencies do not have any proof. **And forcing them to validate removes a large percentage of collections from credit reports. You MUST ask the collection agency that your account be "validated" not just verified. And if that does not work, inform the credit bureaus that the agency has not fulfilled its obligation under the law.**

To understand why, you need to understand the way collections agencies work. They have millions of accounts from which to collect. And they get only a portion of the total amount. So they work on volume. There is no way they can store and handle millions of documents dealing with every account they handle. Even with computers, it is a very hard task.

You can get sample letters to request validation on the Internet at many web sites including *creditboards.com, creditinfocenter.com,* and *creditinsider.com*

The Seven-Year Limit

Collections, like other negative information, are supposed to be removed after seven years. But collection agencies make a habit of breaking this law. **As far as Congress is concerned, the seven-year limit starts 180 days after the account becomes delinquent.** And it does not matter when the collection company got it, or how many different collection companies have had it.

That is the good news. The bad news is that agencies have never followed the letter of the law. It is a ruthless business that does ruthless things. For example, NCO Financial Systems, one of the largest agencies, settled a lawsuit in 2004 for violating the seven-year limit.

Bad debt accounts are normally sold and resold. Every time the account is sold, the new company, usually another collection company, adds a new collection. So the same account might show up more than once. This can be disputed. The collection should only show up once, no matter who owns the right to collect it.

CHAPTER 5

Credit Repair Companies

You've seen the ads all over town: "Guaranteed credit repair!" or "Clean credit in 90 Days!" These ads are put out by credit repair companies.

Credit repair companies are businesses that claim to be able to eliminate negative/derogatory information from a person's credit report. Nowadays, there are even attorneys who offer credit repair services. They say they can miraculously fix your credit and get you all the credit you want, no matter how bad it is. But in order to do this they usually ask for large sums of money. Unfortunately, credit repair companies have a reputation for operating illegally and ripping off their customers. They prey mostly on people with severe credit problems who have nowhere else to turn. These people are told that the repair company knows special tricks or can help them take advantage of special loopholes in the law.

HOT TIP: Credit repair companies are businesses that claim to be able to eliminate negative/derogatory information from your credit report.

Not only is that untrue, but credit repair companies can't do anything that you cannot do yourself.

A word of caution before we begin: do not use the following techniques at home. They are for your education only. We cannot be held responsible if you try these tactics only to make things worse for yourself.

File Segregation

Contrary to their ads, repair companies use common techniques to try to clear credit. One such method is file segregation. With file segregation, the company tries to create a totally new credit file for the consumer. They call this a "new identity" for the consumer.

Here's how it works: The consumer is asked to contact the IRS and apply for an Employer Identification Number (EIN). This number has the same number of digits as a Social Security number. This number is needed and used by employers to report information to the IRS and Social Security Administration. After the consumer has this number, he is told to use it in place of his Social Security number when applying for credit.

When a credit check is done, if it says "no credit record found," that means a new credit file has been created for this customer. Then, whenever the consumer goes to apply for credit, instead of giving his SSN he now gives his EIN. Some credit companies even take it a step further by telling the applicant that after he has the EIN to use it to apply for credit under a name other than his own. For example, a woman could use her maiden name, or a man could use his nickname or middle name as a last name. Applicants will also be told to use a different address than their own on the application.

So the final result is a new person, with a new name, a new address, and a new SSN. I have seen this work and I have also seen this technique backfire. When it does backfire, the person has the

EIN listed on his regular credit report as well as his official SSN. Whenever a creditor (or future creditor) sees two SSNs, it serves as a red flag. In some cases, it does not even take such an elaborate scheme to create a new credit file.

One man I worked with had three separate credit files at the same bureau. All of them had bad credit, but each one had a different first and last name, even though the SSN was the same. The credit bureaus claim their computers would catch something like this, but it is still happening.

The Dispute-A-Thon

The FCRA says that consumers have the right to challenge any item in their credit report they feel is incorrect. It also says that credit bureaus must investigate this matter "within a reasonable period of time." The law has been updated, so that now all disputes must be investigated within 30 days or else they must be deleted by the bureau.

Credit repair companies use this to overload the bureau with so many disputes at the same time that not all can be investigated within the 30 days, and so must be deleted by law. For example, if a person has 15 derogatory accounts on his credit report, the repair company would send letters disputing all 15 accounts at the same time.

This would work except for the fact that the FCRA also states that the bureaus need not investigate claims which are deemed "frivolous" by the bureau. As such, a credit bureau might ignore all 15 disputes. Notice the word *frivolous*. That is the exact word used in the law. But what is frivolous to you might not be frivolous to me, so the bureaus have a lot of room in how they interpret the law.

CREDIT SECRET: Bureaus do not need to investigate claims which are deemed "frivolous."

Repeated Disputes

A third technique is to dispute information over and over gain. For example, let's says the consumer disputed a particular account, but the bureau investigated it and within 30 days sent a letter to the consumer that the account was accurate. The credit repair company would advise the consumer to wait a week or so and dispute it again and, if the bureau again says it is accurate, to dispute it a third time.

The thinking is that since it costs the bureau money each time they investigate something, they might just decide to not investigate it and delete it. Or, the employees of the bureau might get so sick of investigating the same report over and over that they delay working on it so the 30 day time period expires.

Listed below are some of the false claims that credit repair companies have told potential clients in the past.

False Claim: After declaring bankruptcy, you will not be able to get credit for 10 years.

☑ Truth: Ten years is the length of time that the bankruptcy will show up on your credit report. That does not mean you will not be able to get credit for that long. I have seen hundreds of cases where people who filed for bankruptcy had several credit cards only a year or two after they had declared bankruptcy and were now applying for a mortgage to buy a house. Remember, there are hundreds of banks that offer credit cards as well as thousands of companies that will give you credit. Each company has its own guidelines regarding to whom it will give credit and to whom it will not. Some companies might not give credit to anyone with a bankruptcy. Others might wait for a year after you declare bankruptcy before granting credit. The more time passes, the easier it will be for you to get credit.

False Claim: The company or "file segregation" is affiliated with the government.

☑ Truth: The government does not work with any companies or organizations that offer this program or anything similar to it.

False Claim: File segregation is legal.

☑ Truth: File segregation requires you to make an untrue or misleading statement when applying for credit. By law, this is credit fraud. It is a federal crime to misrepresent your SSN. It is also a federal crime to obtain an EIN on false pretenses. Not only that, but if you use the phone or mail to apply for credit, you could be persecuted for mail or wire fraud as well.

False Claim: Only the credit repair company can remove old or inaccurate information.

☑ Truth: Again, this is not true, and you should get enough out of this book so that you will know exactly how to remove any old or inaccurate information. Anything these companies can do for you, you can do for yourself.

The Credit Repair Organization Act

The Credit Repair Organization Act was passed by Congress in September 1996 and went into effect on April 1, 1997. The statute is the first federal law targeting credit repair scams. It applies to companies operating intrastate as well as interstate, and regardless of whether they deal with consumers over the phone. It is enforced by the Federal Trade Commission and state attorney generals.

The most important consumer rights under the law are:

- It prohibits all credit repair companies from taking any money from consumers *before* services are performed.
- It requires credit repair companies to give consumers a written disclosure explaining their legal rights about their credit history *before* any contract is signed.

- It requires credit repair companies to give consumers a written contract with all the terms and conditions of payment, a detailed description of services to be performed (including any guarantees of performance) and an estimate of how long it will take to perform the contract.
- It gives consumers a three-day cooling off period, or right to cancel any agreement they sign with a credit repair company.
- It states that any contract made between a consumer and credit repair company that doesn't comply with the law is void.

Credit repair companies have a history of ripping people off and using illegal tactics. It is for this reason that the Big 3 bureaus refuse to work with credit repair companies. The Big 3 will not sell reports to any credit repair company or attorney. And, if they find out that any of their subscribers are selling reports to credit repair companies, the bureau will cancel that subscriber. Experian seems to be the toughest on this measure. I have received several letters from them warning that such and such company has been doing credit repair and not to deal with them.

Credit repair companies are also calling themselves credit counseling services. If you still decide to use a credit repair company, be careful. One of my friends used a credit repair company to clean his credit. They were successful in getting all derogatory credit off his report (except for one item) but he paid them $6,000 for the service. Also, he told me that they didn't do anything he couldn't have done himself had he had the time. Well, for $6,000 I would have made the time.

CREDIT SECRET: If you find the time, you can do for yourself the same thing a credit repair company will do for you.

Still not convinced? Take some of the following actions if you are still interested in working with one of these companies:

- Call the local Better Business Bureau to ask about any complaint files against this company.
- Call your state's attorney general and ask if there have been any lawsuits or actions taken against this company.
- Never give any money upfront.
- Have them put in writing what they will do.

HOT TIP: Never give any money upfront to a credit repair company.

If You Have Already Been Used and Abused by a Credit Repair Company

Most states have laws regulating these companies. These laws could come in handy if you have lost money. Make sure to report these companies and do not think it is not worth your time. You can make sure these people do not get a chance to rip off others. You need to contact your local Better Business Bureau, your local Consumer Affairs Office, and your state's attorney general. Check with your local directory assistance for their phone numbers. You can also contact the Federal Trade Commission. If you think the company has committed credit fraud, you can write to the FTC at:

Correspondence Branch
Federal Trade Commission
Washington, DC 20580

Another option is to contact the National Fraud Information Center. You can call them at 800-876-7060 or find them online at *www.fraud.org*. They are a private, nonprofit organization that helps people file complaints. They also forward such complaints to the FTC.

HOT TIP: The National Fraud Information Center is a private, nonprofit organization that helps people file complaints.

This news release, put out by Connecticut Attorney General Richard Blumenthal's office, can also be viewed at *http://www.cslib.org/attygenl/mainlinks/tabindex4.htm*

News Release

State, FTC Crack Down on Credit Repair Fraud

Fifteen lawsuits were announced today against credit repair companies, as a result of a joint investigation by the Federal Trade Commission and state attorneys general, including Connecticut Attorney General Richard Blumenthal.

The companies violated federal or state laws designed to protect consumers and were uncovered by the investigation, dubbed "Operation Payback." No Connecticut companies are among those announced today, though Blumenthal filed a similar lawsuit last year against a Stamford-based credit repair company.

"These companies promised the impossible—to make accurate financial information miraculously disappear," Blumenthal said. "Charging for this credit black magic combines insult and injury."

"Credit repair services continue to be a major money maker for boiler room con artists who prey on consumers already in financial trouble and bilk them out of millions of dollars every year," Blumenthal said. "They raise futile hopes that unfavorable financial information can be erased or removed from files, when by law it must be retained." Some of the credit repair companies sued today charged more than $1,000 for services that consumers can perform for themselves for free or at very little cost.

Last May, Blumenthal filed a lawsuit against Credit Resource Management Group of Stamford and in October won a $482,000 judgment against the company, which was accused of cheating consumers with false promises to erase bad credit.

The cases announced today, brought by the FTC, were aimed at enforcing the credit repair provision of the FTC's new Telemarketing Sales Rule. Federal law now makes it illegal for credit repair telemarketers to ask for any money from consumers until six months after they deliver their services.

"Credit repair companies cannot remove accurate, up-to-date information from consumers' credit records," Blumenthal said. "The new telemarketing law gives attorneys general a new tool to combat credit repair scams. If a credit repair company calls you and asks for payment, they are violating the law."

The state received more than 300 complaints from consumers in the case and successfully froze the company's bank accounts. The company charged a $95 start-up fee and cost consumers as much as $1,400.

The FTC announced four actions today:

- The Law Center and The Consumer Law Center, two names under which Walter D. Channels and James Martin Coose of southern California, have done credit repair business. These defendants charged consumers $1,000 or more, requested at least partial payment up front.
- Giving You Credit Inc. and Partners in Vision International, both of San Diego, and Clear Your Credit of Chicago, which allegedly charged tens of thousands of consumers up to $520 each. The defendants in this case have agreed to settle the charges under a consent decree that prohibits them from engaging in similar practices and requires them to notify customers that they are not required to make any

more payments and to cease all collection efforts against customers.

- Jayco Associates Inc., doing business as Credit Doctor of Washington, D.C., which allegedly charged consumers as much as $995 up front for its services and claimed to have as many as 18,000 clients. Jayco agreed to pay $15,000 to be used for refunds to customers who were victims of the firm's alleged violations. The judgment also prohibits them from trying to collect payment on past contracts and requires them to withdraw negative reports they sent to credit reporting agencies.
- A fourth case against a California company was filed under seal and the seal has not been lifted by the court.

In addition, attorneys general in nine states and the District of Columbia filed other actions against credit repair companies, including DTM Financial Services of Walpole, Mass., Midwell Financial Services of Wakefield, N.H., and National Credit Management Group of Fort Lee, N.J.

Blumenthal urged any Connecticut consumer who may have done business with any of the credit repair companies named in the crackdown—or any other believed to have violated the telemarketing rule—to contact his office.

CHAPTER 6

Getting Credit

▶Your Right to Credit—the ECOA

The Equal Credit Opportunity Act (ECOA) is the statute that regulates the credit evaluation and application process. The ECOA was created to prevent discrimination.

It prevents creditors from rejecting your application for credit because of your:

- age
- marital status
- national origin
- race/color
- religion
- sex

Age—Age was added primarily to protect the elderly. Creditors can grant credit to minors, but they usually stay away from this practice. It is illegal to turn someone down for credit based solely on their age.

- Credit scoring systems cannot give lower scores based on age.
- Pensions, Social Security and annuities must be counted as income when evaluating the application.
- The status and terms of your accounts and loans cannot be changed solely because you reach a certain age or retire.

Marital status—The ECOA allows you to get credit in your name only. The creditor cannot ask you to have a spouse or someone else cosign simply because you are married.

The only time a creditor can ask you of your marital status is:

- When you pay alimony or child support/or are listing it as income.
- When you list your spouse's income as an income source in order to qualify.
- In the event your spouse will use the account.
- You live in a community property state or are listing property that is in a community property state. These states are Arizona, California, Idaho, Louisiana, Nevada, New Mexico, Texas, Washington, and Wisconsin.

A creditor cannot cancel your account or change the terms if your marital status changes, as long as you continue to qualify for the loan. If the account is a joint account and you get divorced, the creditor can ask you to reapply for the account under your own name, but they cannot cancel or freeze the account while you are trying to do this.

In community property states, the property you own is also owned by your spouse. Therefore creditors have more authority in asking you questions about your marital situation and your spouse.

National Origin—You cannot be denied credit or given different terms based on where you were born.

HOT TIP: The ECOA does not forbid creditors from denying credit to nonpermanent residents or aliens.

Race/Color—Creditors are prohibited from asking you your race or color on an application. The only exception is when you apply for a mortgage. For government monitoring purposes, the loan officer can ask you your race, but must also tell you that you do not have to answer. If you refuse, the loan officer is required by law to answer for you based on personal observation.

Sex

- It is optional for you to fill out the title on an application (Mr. Ms, Miss, or Mrs.).
- Women must be given the same credit and terms as a man with similar qualifications.
- Pregnant women can also not be discriminated against for credit.

Other Rights

It is to safeguard the public against discrimination that the ECOA contains the rule that creditors have 30 days to tell you if your application was accepted or rejected. Credit approval can take from seconds to a couple of weeks, depending on the type of credit. If you do not hear anything from the lender within 30 days, be sure to give them a call.

If you are extended credit other than what you applied for, you have the right to refuse it. This happens most with credit cards. If you apply for a gold card with a credit limit of $10,000 and you receive instead a standard card with a limit of $4,000, you can refuse the card even though you applied for it. Be sure not to activate it.

Cut it up and throw it away. To be sure, call the company and tell them you've refused their card. The account should not show up on your credit report, but the inquiry will.

HOT TIP: If you receive a credit card you do not want, cut it up and throw it away.

What Do You Do When You Get Rejected?

If you are rejected for credit, you have the right (under the ECOA) to know the specific reason why you were denied credit. You also have the right to know the name of the bureau that supplied the credit report. Under the FCRA, you are entitled to a free credit report from that bureau within 60 days of your denial. It is a good idea to always request this free report. It cost you nothing and you get to check if anything is on it that doesn't belong.

Rejection letters are usually form letters. They say something to the effect of "Sorry, we are unable to grant you the credit you applied for because of such and such reasons. We used a credit report from the bureau listed below to check your credit. You may contact them for a free copy of your report."

Some companies do not list the reason for your credit denial on the rejection letter. Note that this is not illegal. You will have to contact the company and ask for the reason.

CREDIT SECRET: You only have 60 days to contact a company regarding your credit rejection.

An address or toll free number should be listed on the letter. You should also contact the company if any reasons for rejection are not specified on the letter, or if you do not understand them. The law says the reasons must be specific, but exactly how specific is a matter of interpretation.

Regardless of what the law says, creditors will try to be as vague as possible in their rejections. The reason is that creditors are afraid of being sued by consumers who are wrongly turned down. In order to avoid lawsuits, creditors will try to use general terms. An example would be if one of the reasons was "number of revolving accounts." If you receive that as a reason for rejection, you would likely have no idea what it meant. Do you have too few or too many accounts? Usually it is too many, but if so, how many is too many? Creditors do not give explanations unless you call them and confront them.

If you do get rejected, do not get discouraged. There are plenty of companies out there who are dying to give you credit. It is your job to find them. But if you want credit from a company that rejected you, you still have a few options. The first steps are to find out why you were rejected and to fully understand the reasons behind the rejection. If it was due to derogatory credit, explain your side of the story. If you already have too much credit, tell them you are willing to close some accounts. Ask the rep what you should do to get accepted. Take the necessary steps to overcome the rejection's reason. If your report has inaccurate information, get that fixed and apply again.

HOT TIP: If you feel you have rectified the reason for your rejections and they still do not issue you credit, you have one more tool.

If you feel you have rectified the reason for your rejections and they still do not issue you credit, you have one more tool. You should write a letter to the company explaining everything that occurred during your application process. Attach a copy of your rejection letter, listing what actions you took to fix the situation or the circumstances that were not under your control. Explain why you feel you would be a responsible customer. **Send this letter to the company and send a copy of the letter to the company's legal department. Address it to the compliance officer.** Not too many people go this route, and therefore you can be assured that you will receive a response.

If you already have a credit card and are refused an increase in your credit limit, you have the same rights as listed above. You must be told the specific reasons why you were refused and you can receive a free copy of your report if they check your credit.

If the terms of your account are changed by the creditor, you must be notified within 30 days of the changes and you must be given the reason why.

Building Credit for the First Time

Having no credit is not as bad as most people make it out to be. In fact, getting credit is not really very hard to do. If you make decent money, there is someone out there who would be very happy to lend you money. So don't worry about it.

HOT TIP: Getting credit for the first time is really rather simple to do.

This section will outline:

- Ways to get credit if you do not have any now
- How to apply for credit
- What credit you should apply for first
- How to get the credit card you want
- A real life case study

Nowadays, with credit applications flooding mailboxes across the U.S., it is hard to imagine anyone without credit. But if you happen to be one of these rare individuals, you are better off than those who are trying to rebuild their credit. You have a blank slate. You have no record, and companies are willing to bet that you will be responsible and pay them back. We need to use this to your advantage.

The people who most likely do not have any credit are:

- Youngsters—mainly teenagers and those in their early twenties
- Recently divorced women—who let their husbands handle the finances
- The elderly—who have not used credit for several years
- Recent immigrants

The Young

The majority of those who have no credit are young people. For them, it is easy to get credit since they are just starting out in life, are upwardly mobile and have salaries that should be increasing as they grow older.

If you are a college student, you should have no problem getting credit. Credit card applications are plastered all over most universities and colleges in the country. The major banks are falling all over each other offering credit to students. You do not even need any income; just fill out the application and you most likely will be accepted.

HOT TIP: If you are a college student, you should have no problem getting credit.

In most university courtyards, companies set up tables in the courtyard and give away free stuff like t-shirts or chocolate bars as bribes for filling out an application. In fact, there are actually companies that specialize in this. They are hired by the banks to get kids to fill out credit applications. These companies get paid for each completed application they turn in to the bank. If you miss them at school, you can probably find them at the airport where they also set up tables.

With so much competition in the credit industry, it is hard for banks to find new markets. Students are the perfect targets. Not only are most students willing to get more than one card, but research shows that the majority of people keep their credit cards for several years. So the banks try to get them while they are young. And the banks are not really worried about the payments either, especially since parents usually get involved and pay the bill if the kid gets in over his head (which happens a lot).

HOT TIP: Students are the perfect targets for banks trying to find new markets.

If you are a parent with a son or daughter in high school or above, it is extremely important to discuss the benefits and pitfalls of credit, so that they use it responsibly. This is what my parents did with me. I got my first Visa at age 17 (while still in high school), but I was not allowed to use it unless it was an emergency. I never really used it until I got to college anyway, but can you imagine a bank offering cards to kids in high school?

The Divorced

If you have recently gotten divorced, chances are that you already have credit and that some of it is bad. But if you do not, it is actually a good thing. In most divorce cases that I have seen, the couple has several joint credit accounts that still have outstanding balances when they divorce. As part of the divorce agreement, one spouse agrees to make the payments on that account, but the other spouse is still liable since it is a joint account. Eventually, the payments are not made and both spouses' credit is negatively affected.

If you do not have any joint accounts, consider yourself lucky. You will have no trouble getting yourself some credit in a short amount of time.

The Elderly

After several years of earning, saving and paying the bills, how is it possible that the elderly would have no credit?

Even if you have had credit before, if you haven't used it for over seven years, it will be taken off your record. At this point, you once again have no credit. What this means is, if you have not purchased anything on credit in the past seven years, your credit report has been cleared. Everything should have been taken off...all the good and all the bad.

CREDIT SECRET: If you haven't used your credit for over seven years, it will be taken off your record.

I once helped an older gentleman who had been out of the country for 10 years. Imagine his surprise when he found it difficult to obtain credit, because he now had no credit history in his file. Since he was out of the country, he had not used his credit and had to start all over again.

Immigrants

As long as you have a Social Security number, you can get credit. There are thousands of immigrants in the U.S. who have had the ability to get credit, and then mess it up. So when you get it, take it seriously.

All the techniques that are discussed in the next chapter, **Creating Good Credit** chapter can work for someone with no credit. So please be sure to read that chapter. Just by using only a couple of the strategies contained within that chapter you could obtain thousands of dollars worth of credit pretty easily.

Applying for Credit

When you first apply for credit, the lender will have you fill out an application. From the information contained in that application and by reviewing a copy of your credit report, the lender will determine if it wants to extend credit to you.

CREDIT SECRET: Lenders look at five major factors when deciding whether or not to extend credit to you.

The major factors lenders look at are:

1. Your income—the more the better.
2. How long you have been at your present job—the longer the better.
3. How long you have been at your present address—the longer the better.
4. How much you owe in liabilities—the lower the better.
5. Past credit history

By combining all these factors, the lender will determine if you meet its standards for the amount of credit you requested.

The following is a list of different types of credit, ranked in order from easiest to hardest to obtain:

1. Co-signed credit card or loans
2. Secured cards

3. Local store credit—furniture, used car dealerships, appliance stores
4. National department store cards
5. Gas cards
6. Cellular phones
7. Visa/MasterCard/Discover
8. American Express
9. Car loans
10. Home mortgages

When you start to apply for credit, do not apply for too much credit in a short amount of time. Every time someone checks your credit, an inquiry shows up on your report. These inquiries could cause you to be rejected. The more inquires you have, the more desperate for credit you seem. And if you are desperate for credit, then no one will want to lend you money. Too many inquires also lowers your credit score if you already have one.

HOT TIP: If you appear desperate for credit, then no one will want to lend you money.

When you fill out a credit application, it is important to remember that lying is illegal. There is no way to really get caught, but if further down the road you run into financial difficulty, it could come back to haunt you if you do not pay on time and declare bankruptcy. At the bankruptcy hearing, the creditors will charge that you committed fraud by lying. So be as truthful on applications as possible.

Most credit card applications are simple enough. They ask for your name, address, Social Security number, household income, phone number, work phone number, mother's maiden name, and signature. Make sure you get the name, address and Social Security right and that the information is clear.

HOT TIP: Your household income is the total amount that everyone in your house earns.

Your household income is the total amount that everyone in your house earns.

That means you should add up how much you, your spouse, your parents, your children, and anyone else in your house earn. This will be a much greater amount than if you only wrote down the total of your own personal income, and this will make you a much more attractive credit applicant. Be sure to NEVER understate your income. It is usually the most important factor when you have no credit.

As for your phone numbers, I advise all my clients to not give the credit card companies their true phone numbers. I advise that you should alter your real home phone number by one digit and give this number out to anyone who requests it whom you do not want to give your real number to. You probably never want these people calling you at work, so you can give them your fax number instead of your work phone number.

The credit card companies do not need your phone number. If they want to get in touch with you, let them mail you a letter. The only reason they want your phone number is to call you when you miss a payment and to sell your number to telemarketers. Do you really want people calling you to either tell you to pay them or to sell you something you do not want? Neither do I.

CREDIT SECRET: The above technique makes sure that you will never get called by a telemarketer again. Use it well.

When they ask for your mother's maiden name, it is used as a password. Instead, make up your own password and give them that.

When you call about your account, the bank will not talk to you unless you know this password.

CREDIT SECRET: Instead of giving them your mother's maiden name, make up your own password.

Your mother's name could be easily found by anyone with a computer. If you are creative, you can make up a word and use that. "Masasagua…" that would be hard for any crook to guess.

REAL LIFE CASE STUDY: In order to maintain his privacy, I will not reveal his name, but the following story is about a client of mine whom I helped get great credit within one year. Let's call him "Bob." Bob is an immigrant. He came to the U.S. with his family on a short-term Immigration Visa. He is allowed to stay here for five years, and if he wants to stay longer, he must apply for an extension.

When he got here, he got his driver's license and his Social Security card. At first, his main source of information about how things work in the U.S. was from his relatives who had lived in the States. They told him it was important to get credit and that it was also very hard to get, especially for immigrants new to the country.

After a few months, Bob and his family settled down here in Houston. They had an apartment and checking account, and bought a used car (all paid for with cash). Yet Bob still couldn't get credit, so he came to see me.

The first thing I had Bob do was go to the bank where he had his checking account, Bank of America, and apply for a secured card. They asked him to deposit $500 into a separate account and gave him a secured card with a $500 limit. After 6 months, if he paid on time, they would up his limit to $1,000. After one year, they would convert the card to an unsecured card and he could take his $500 back.

I advised Bob to use his new card for small purchases, like groceries and gas for his car. When the bill came, he paid it in full. Within a couple months, Bob had great credit and the offers started to arrive...lots of them. Every week, Bob started to get a pre-approved offer for one credit card or another. Some were for secured cards, but others were for unsecured cards, the ones he wanted. He applied for one at a time. The first one gave him a limit of $500, not much, but better than nothing. The second gave him a limit of $2,000. After six months, Bob was able to cancel the Bank of America secured card, get his $500 back and had over $10,000 worth of unsecured credit. We only applied for the cards with no annual fees, generous grace periods and low interest rates. The last time I heard from Bob, he was shopping for a new car and was already approved for a loan.

You too, can be just like "Bob."

CHAPTER 7

Creating Good Credit

The best way to improve your credit is to add some good credit to your report. This is not as hard as it sounds. Even if you have horrible credit and your own mother won't lend you five dollars, there is still hope. Whether you are rebuilding your credit or starting out and establishing your credit for the first time, this chapter will show you numerous ways you can get credit within a couple of weeks.

HOT TIP: This chapter will show you numerous ways you can get credit within a couple of weeks.

This chapter is all about creating new accounts that can be added to your credit report in order to: a) improve your credit score; and b) show to creditors that you are not a deadbeat and do want to be financially responsible. In this chapter we will discuss:

- Adding non-reported accounts to your report
- Being an authorized user —this is the easiest and fastest way to improve your credit

- The bank loan-a-thon
- Secured cards
- Co-signing

Adding Non-Reported Accounts to Your Report

Did you know that you already have credit? Your utilities, your insurance, and your used car payments are examples of credit that usually do not show up on credit reports. These companies do not want to go through the hassle and expense of reporting your account to the credit bureaus every month, but you can make them. According to federal law, if your credit report contains information that causes you to be denied for credit, you have the right to add positive information to your report.

Certain creditors want to report your accounts and to do this they spend a lot of money submitting that information to the credit bureaus every month. Other creditors do not do this unless you do not pay. When you do not pay, they will report the account as a negative to the credit bureaus.

In order to add a non-reported account to your report, you need to contact the credit bureaus and give them a list of businesses with which you do business and which extend you credit. The bureaus then call these companies and ask for a reference on your account. These accounts will then be added to your file.

CREDIT SECRET: There is a fee involved in adding non-reported accounts to your file and it varies from bureau to bureau.

These accounts will also not be updated every month. Be sure to give them only a list of businesses with which you have had no credit problems.

A list of such places would be:

- Phone company
- Electric company
- Gas company
- Used car finance company
- Insurance company
- Furniture rental company.

Honestly, this method is the biggest headache. If you can use the other methods first, do so, and leave this for last resort.

Authorized User

How would you like to have an account added to your credit report that has been opened for years, has a very high limit and has never been late? How would you like to have dozens of accounts like this? Read on, my friend.

The best way I know of establishing good credit is to use someone else's. This sounds illegal but it is the easiest and fastest way to build up your credit. All you need to do is find a friend or relative with good credit who trusts you enough to help you. Actually, they do not even have to trust you that much. They just have to be willing to help you.

CREDIT SECRET: To establish good credit yourself, all you need to do is find a friend or relative with existing good credit who trusts you enough to help you.

This person can add you to all of his credit and store cards as an authorized user. All of the accounts are now automatically added to you credit file...quickly and painlessly. Your friend calls the credit card company and says that he wants to add you to his account as an authorized user. They ask for your information. They then send him a card for that account with your name on it. That account then gets posted to your credit and updated every month.

An authorized user is allowed to use the account but is not responsible for payment. This makes it hard to find someone willing to agree to such an arrangement but it is not impossible. The accounts will list that you are an authorized user but everything else will be the same.

Technically, you would be able to use the account, but this is not what you want to do. Once your friend gets the card with your name, he can keep it to make sure you do not use it. The more time goes by, the better your credit gets. Your friend keeps using his account as usual. He still has to make the payments. If your friend starts paying late, however, those late payments will show up on your report too, even though you are not responsible for payment.

The whole process takes about two weeks. Once you have one or two of these accounts, monitor your credit score and watch it improve. You should then be able to apply for and get your own credit cards in a short amount of time.

I personally did this for a friend of mine. He was starting out with no credit whatsoever. So I called Citibank and got him added to my credit card. I kept the card, and he stayed as an authorized user for about a year. Within six months, he was able to get his own credit and I was able to have him removed as an authorized user. It helped him out and all it took was a phone call.

The Bank Loan-A-Thon

With this technique, you use your own money to get several bank loans. My father used this method when he first moved to this country. It is fairly simple but you need to tell the banks what you are doing.

First, take $1,000 (or an amount close to it) and open a passbook savings account in a bank. Tell your banker you want to take a loan out against the money to establish your credit. Wait a few days for the account to be posted then go back and get a short-term 5–6 month loan. Try to get the bank to waive any interest charges.

Second, you take the money borrowed from the loan and deposit it in another bank then repeat the whole process. Do this at 4–5 banks and you will have many positive bank loans on your credit. At the last bank, open a checking account if you do not already have one and begin making payments on your loans. After 4–5 months pay them all off.

Use banks that have free checking accounts. And before you open the account, ask them if they can help you get a short-term loan using the money in your account as collateral. If the person opening the account does not know, then get them to ask the manager. If they do not do these kinds of loans then you need to go to another bank.

Thankfully, most large cities have several banks to choose from and the branch you go to also makes a difference. I have had clients get turned down at one branch and then open the same account at another branch. I have no clue why. Banks are funny places, so keep trying.

Nowadays, larger banks are using large database companies like Telecheck to see if you have written bad checks before. This information can stay in the database for years. It is like a credit report of bank accounts. And to tell you the truth, many times it is just a scam.

PERSONAL STORY: After we moved to Houston from Miami, I opened three different checking accounts at a local bank. A year later, I went in to open another account. The bank had recently started using Telecheck. Even though I was a good customer and have never written a bad check, they refused to open another bank account for me because of something negative against me in the Telecheck database. I was told to contact Telecheck to straighten it out.

Well, I called them and listened to their computer for a long, long time. The only thing I could get was that they said I owed money to the bank I had a personal account with in Miami, which was totally untrue. After waiting on hold for over an hour to talk to someone, I gave up. I tried calling Telecheck over ten times to talk to someone in an attempt to find out what this charge was and what it was for. Forget about it! What I eventually ended up doing was using a computer option that lets you pay the debt by credit card, all done electronically. I did not have time to waste with this lousy company and thus was forced to pay them over $60 for a false claim. They basically blackmailed me for $60. I called over ten times and never talked to a human. Hopefully you do not have to go through this type of scam.

Secured Cards

A secured card is a good tool to help you rebuild your credit, or build it for the first time. A secured card is a bank granted credit card that is backed by a deposit of collateral at the bank. To be approved for the secured card, all you need to do is make a security deposit at the bank. The bank then issues you a Visa or MasterCard with a spending limit equal to the money you placed in deposit. Note that you will not be allowed to touch the money in the account as long as you have the card. If you do not pay your bills, the bank will seize the money in your account as payment. They will then close your account.

HOT TIP: A secured card is a good tool to help you rebuild your credit.

Even secured cards have minimum standards. Thus, most issuers ask you to fill out an application and check your credit prior to approval. There are companies that guarantee cards to anyone as long as you pay a fee. All these companies do is send you a list of banks that offer the cards. In the past, scam artists found it easy to prey on individuals who were desperate for credit. There still are many con artists out there, but there has been a renewed interest in this industry and more and more legitimate issuers are coming on the scene. The best place to start looking for a secured card is the bank at which you have a checking account. If you do not have a checking account, start at the largest bank in your neighborhood.

Secured cards look just like regular bankcards. No one can tell that the card is secured. You are expected to make regular payments. If you do so, the issuer might convert your account to an unsecured card in 1 to 7 years time. Alternatively, the issuer might only increase your limit to a higher amount than what you have in deposit. It all really depends on the bank. Secured cards also show up on you credit report, just like normal bank cards, except they are marked with a code that means secured. Most creditors do not differentiate much between secured and regular bankcards. This makes it easier for you to qualify for other cards.

On the other hand, if you do not pay your bills, you will ruin your credit even more, and the bank will put your account in collections. They will not touch the deposit unless all other means of payment have been exhausted, and they, or you, cancel the account.

Because of the popularity of secured cards, many secured card scams have appeared in the marketplace, so you need to be on the lookout for them.

The following tips will help you determine if a secured card ad is legitimate:

- In the advertisement, the name of the bank that is issuing the card will be stated. Visa and MasterCard both require all marketers to name the issuing bank in all ads. If no bank is mentioned, look elsewhere.
- If they promise a "guaranteed" Visa or MasterCard, it might be a scam. No one can guarantee a bankcard. There are many factors that could cause several card issuers to reject applications.
- The deposit must be held in an account that is protected by the Federal Deposit Insurance Corporation (FDIC). If it is not and the bank goes out of business, you could lose all your money. The FDIC protects savings accounts up to $100,000.

HOT TIP: There are several questions to ask the issuing bank about before applying for a secured credit card.

The number one question you should ask is whether or not the account will be reported to the three bureaus. If your account will not be reported, it is not worth your time if you are trying to rebuild or build your credit. If the bank reports to one or two bureaus only, ask them to report your account to the remaining ones.

The second question to ask is whether or not the account will be reported as a secured account. Some issuers do not report the account as secured while most do. If you can get them not to report it as secured, it is in your best interest.

Other factors you need to know about are the amount you will be required to put in deposit, the interest rate you will earn on that deposit, what percentage of your deposit will comprise your card's spending limit and any processing or application fees.

HOT TIP: Make sure you know what percentage of your deposit will comprise your card's spending limit.

Cosigning

If you are building or rebuilding your credit, you might want someone to cosign a loan with you, or you might be asked by someone to cosign on their loan. If you cosign the loan, you agree to pay back the total amount of the loan if the primary borrower does not pay. You become legally responsible for that debt. If the debt is not paid, your credit will be ruined, you will be placed in collection, and you can even be sued by the creditor. The creditor is not required to inform the cosigner that the account is not being paid as agreed.

HOT TIP: If you cosign a loan, you agree to pay back the total amount of the loan if the primary borrower does not pay.

Cosigning for someone else can also hurt you when applying for credit yourself. If information about the cosigned account is negative, it will count against you even though it is not supposed to be your account. Also, lenders take the payments of the cosigned account into consideration when calculating your total liabilities. They might decide that you have too much credit already. They want to be sure that you will be able to make the payments on both your accounts and the cosigned accounts in case you have to.

If you are going to cosign for someone else, ask yourself some questions first:

- Is the person responsible enough and capable of making the payments?

- If the person does not make the payments, can you afford to make them for the life of the loan?
- How large is the loan amount? Can it hurt you when you apply for credit yourself?

Cosigning is a commonly used tactic but I do not recommend it. If you are asking someone to cosign for you to improve your credit, know that there are much better ways to do so, and these have already been outlined in this chapter. If someone asks you to cosign, you might actually be hurting them by helping them get a loan that they cannot handle financially. If you still want to cosign for someone else, you might consider taking out the loan as the primary borrower and having the other person cosign the loan. That way the bills come to you. This will make it easier for you to make sure the payments are being made.

CHAPTER 8

The Credit Score

Recently the popularity of credit bureau scores has increased dramatically. Most large lenders have their own scoring systems. Each bureau has its own risk score. The score is a grading of how risky you are as a client. The higher your score, the less risky you are.

Experian has teamed up with the Fair Isaac companies to offer the "FICO score." Equifax offers the "Beacon score," while TransUnion offers the "Emperica score." All the models are fairly similar. They all grade using the same factors but they place different amounts of importance on different factors. That is one of the reasons your score for each one will be different. The point range that is used is from the 300s to the mid 800s.

CREDIT SECRET: All three credit bureaus grade your creditworthiness using similar factors.

Experian score factors:

01	Current balances on account
02	Delinquency reported on accounts
03	Too few bank revolving accounts
04	Too many bank revolving accounts
05	Number of accounts with balances
06	Number of finance company accounts
07	Unable to evaluate recent payment history
08	Number of recent inquiries
33	Proportion of current loan balance to original loan amount
09	Number of accounts opened within the last twelve months
10	Proportion of balance to high credit on bank revolving or all revolving accounts
11	Current balances on revolving accounts
12	Length of revolving account history
13	Length of time (or unknown time) since account delinquency
14	Length of time accounts have been established
15	Insufficient or lack of bank revolving account information
16	Insufficient or lack of revolving account information
17	No recent (non-mortgage) account balance information
18	Number of accounts delinquent
19	Too few accounts rated "current"
24	Lack of recently reported balances on revolving/open accounts
20	Length of time since legal item filed or collection item reported

21	Amount past due to accounts
22	Account(s) not paid as agreed and/or legal item filed
32	No recent installment loan information
30	Length of time since most recent account established
37	Number of finance company accounts established relative to length of finance history
25	Length of installment loan history
26	Number of revolving accounts
99	Lack of recent information on finance accounts or lack of finance accounts
31	Too few accounts with recent payment information
28	Number of accounts established
98	Lack of recent information on auto loan or lack of auto loans
36	Length of time open installment loans have been established

Notice that all the above factors are negative. When a credit grantor asks for your score it will look like the following:

FICO score: 615   Factors: 22, 18, 12, 1
Accounts not paid as agreed and/or legal item filed
Number of accounts delinquent
Length of revolving account history
Current balances on accounts

Your score, with up to four factors, is given. Three factors are given in the order in which they affect your score. The first factor is the most important, the second the second most important and so on. The codes appear in order of relative importance and are followed by the specific factors that most significantly contribute to your score.

HOT TIP: The codes appear in order of relative importance.

You start off with a perfect score. The computer then goes through all of the factors, taking off points for those in which you do not match their ideal customer. The factors listed are the main reasons why your score is lower than the perfect score.

According to TRW (now Experian) printed material, "the TRW/Fair Isaac Model was developed from a representative sample, which consisted of three quarters of a million TRW consumer credit histories." It converts the experience of credit grantors and collection agencies as well as public record information and the inquiries found on a consumer's TRW credit profile report into a numeric score that predicts future behavior.

Using extensive data elements, Fair Isaac analyzed the performance of sample credit histories over a 24-month period. Those variables which most accurately predicted the subsequent credit performance became the basis for scorecard development.

The result is a detailed, highly predictive model consisting of 10 individually targeted scorecards. Each TRW Credit Profile is directed towards a particular scorecard based on the characteristics present on the report. These include:

- Amount of trade lines
- Length of time accounts were open
- Presence of derogatory information

How does your score affect you?

Scores are used for several reasons; some are:

- Pre-screening of credit cards
- Getting initial loan amounts
- Over-limit purchase authorizations
- Credit limit increases
- Determining reissue periods
- Prioritize collections
- Determining how much you pay for insurance

This is but a short list of the uses credit card companies have come up with for credit scores.

Credit scoring also plays a huge role in the mortgage industry. Mortgage lenders are now asking for credit scores on all applications. Currently it is a Fannie Mae requirement that an applicant have a FICO score of at least 620 for the loan to be bought by their organization.

HOT TIP: Credit scoring also plays a huge role in the mortgage industry.

Fannie Mae is a secondary market lender. Most banks and mortgage lenders lend money to you initially and then sell your mortgage as part of a group of mortgages on the secondary market. For example, a few months after most people get their mortgage, they get a letter saying that the mortgage has been bought by ABC Money Co. and that payments should be made to that company from now on. That is an example of a loan being sold. Fannie Mae is a very large buyer of mortgages on the secondary market. They mainly purchases loans from people who have a score of 620 or better. Since it is easy to resell a mortgage belonging to someone with a score of 620, anyone scoring 620 or higher will get good interest rates and anyone with over 720 will get the best rates available.

These are called conforming loans. Of course each lender is different and these guidelines are not set in stone.

People applying for non-conforming loans pay more in interest, simply because their loan is more difficult to sell on the secondary market. That is because they are seen as a credit risk since their credit score is not high enough.

CREDIT SECRET: Anyone scoring 720 or higher will get the best interest rates available.

So how do you find out what your score is?

You can get your score from the bureau. Until recently, bureaus did not give consumers their own scores and forbade any reseller to sell a consumer his/her score. But with the changes to the FCRA in 2004 this has changed.

You can get your score directly from the bureaus, or from other companies and websites such as *www.myfico.com*. This site is run by Fair Issac Co. so you know you are getting your original FICO score. Other sites sell scores based on their computer models but they are not your real FICO score.

How do you improve your score?

You can improve you score pretty easily. In fact, improving your credit score is the same thing as improving your credit. Here are some pointers:

- The longer your accounts have been open the better your score.
- The fewer the number of inquiries within the past 12 months the better your score.
- The less derogatory information you have the better your score.

- The lower the balance on your open accounts the better your score.
- Too few or too many open credit card accounts could lower your score. Zero credit cards is too few, more than 5 is usually too many.
- The fewer the number of new accounts opened with the past 12 months, the better your score.

Do the bureaus give the same score?

Not at all. All three bureaus have different information on their credit reports. As a result, your credit score will be different for each bureau. From my experience, we noticed that TransUnions' Emperica score is usually the most lenient and is usually the highest score of the three. The Experian score comes in second and Equifax's score comes in third. Each person is different, so this order could flip flop, depending on the person, but it is usually in this order.

I have seen credit scores differ by almost 100 points from one bureau to the next. So, if you find out you have been rejected for an account or a loan because your score was too low then ask them to get another score. You might be pleasantly surprised to be approved for the loan. If you are using a mortgage broker to get a mortgage, they will usually do this for you. If they do not, find another broker. But remember the new broker will pull your report once again, meaning another inquiry and in turn resulting in a lower score. It is a Catch-22 situation.

CREDIT SECRET: Each person is different, so the order of your credit scores could flip flop.

How reliable is the credit scoring system?

Credit scoring systems enable creditors to evaluate millions of applicants consistently and impartially on many different characteristics. But to be statistically valid, credit scoring systems must be based on a big enough sample. Remember that these systems generally vary from creditor to creditor.

Although you may think such a system is arbitrary or impersonal, it can help make decisions faster, more accurately, and more impartially than individuals when it is properly designed. And many creditors design their systems so that applicants whose scores are not high enough to pass easily or are low enough to fail absolutely are referred to a credit manager who decides whether the company or lender will extend credit. This may allow for discussion and negotiation between the credit manager and the consumer.

What happens if you are denied credit or don't get the terms you want?

If you are denied credit, the Equal Credit Opportunity Act requires that the creditor give you a notice that tells you the specific reasons your application was rejected or the fact that you have the right to learn the reasons if you ask within 60 days. Indefinite and vague reasons for denial are illegal, so ask the creditor to be specific. Acceptable reasons include: "Your income was low" or "You haven't been employed long enough." Unacceptable reasons include: "You didn't meet our minimum standards" or "You didn't receive enough points on our credit scoring system."

If a creditor says you were denied credit because you are too near your credit limits on your charge cards or you have too many credit card accounts, you may want to reapply after paying down your balances or closing some accounts. Credit scoring systems consider updated information and changes over time.

Sometimes you can be denied credit because of information from a credit report. If so, the Fair Credit Reporting Act requires the creditor to give you the name, address and phone number of the credit reporting agency that supplied the information. You should contact that agency to find out what your report said. This information is free if you request it within 60 days of being turned down for credit. The credit reporting agency can tell you what's in your report, but only the creditor can tell you why your application was denied.

If you have been denied credit, or didn't get the rate or credit terms you want, ask the creditor if a credit scoring system was used. If so, ask what characteristics or factors were used in that system, and the best ways to improve your application. If you get credit, ask the creditor whether you are getting the best rate and terms available and, if not, why. If you are not offered the best rate available because of inaccuracies in your credit report, be sure to dispute the inaccurate information in your credit report.

Why even have a credit scoring system?

Credit scoring is more for lenders than for us normal people. They were created to help lenders determine how risky we are as borrowers. In fact, they were created to do the following:

- Detect fraud in credit and insurance applications
- Determine the amount of profit a bank is likely to make on a credit card account
- Give predictions for different types of defaults, such as collection or bankruptcy.
- Forecast the probability of an insured making too many claims
- Estimate how much a borrower is likely to pay on a bad debt
- Predict the likelihood that someone will respond to a credit card offer

How good is my score?

The higher the score, the better. Different lenders have different cutoffs. So you might be able to get a credit card with a 600 score at one bank, but not at another.

Here is a national distribution chart of FICO scores.

FICO Score	Percentage of US population with this score
300–499	1%
500–549	5%
550–599	7%
600–649	11%
650–699	16%
700–749	20%
750–799	29%
800–850	11%

Everything in your credit report is taken into account when the models create your create score. All the good and all the bad. But greater emphasis is placed on the bad. According to Liz Weston, author of *Your Credit Score,* there are five main factors that affect your score.

1. Payment History. This makes up 35% of your credit score. The more recent any late payments the more your score suffers. Frequent late payments also hurt your score more. And the later the payment the more of a hit your score will take. A late payment 3 years ago is better than one last month. One 30 day late is better than 5. And a 30 day late is better than a 90 day late. According to Fair Isaac, 60% of Americans do not have a single late payment on their credit.
2. Amount Owed. This makes up 30% of your score. The more you owe the worse your score. According to Fair Issac, the average American uses up to 32% of their credit limit.

3. Length of Credit. This is 15% of your score. The longer you have had credit the better. According to Fair Isaac, the average American has had credit for 14 years. The older your accounts are higher your score can go.
4. Inquires and New Accounts. These count for 10% of your score. The more you have, the worse your score. According to Fair Isaac, the average American has not opened a new account in 20 months.
5. Types of Credit. This accounts for 10% of your score. The more varied the better. If you have both revolving (credit cards) and installment (mortgage, car payment, etc.) accounts you are better off than by just having one type. According to Fair Isaac, the average American has four or five bankcards and one installment loan.

How Do I Raise My Credit Score?

To raise your score you need to improve your credit. Do all the things I advised you earlier in the book. Here are the top 7 ways. If you do just these seven, you will see your score raise several points. And almost everyone can use these seven steps.

1. Dispute and remove any derogatory information, especially if it is true.
2. Pay down your balances as much as you can.
3. Consolidate your debts into one account.
4. Stop applying for more credit.
5. Let time work its magic. The more time goes by, after an inquiry, late payment, or collection hits your report, the less it impacts your score.
6. Close your accounts with less than desirable creditors. Consumer finance companies that charge more than normal rates are looked down upon by the credit score models.
7. Keep paying your bills on time.

Once you get your credit score, you will see the remarks and the top reasons why your credit score is suffering. Whatever the reason is, takes steps to fix it. If the reason is you do not have enough revolving accounts, visit your bank and see how you can get one. If the top factor is that you can too many inquires, then stop applying for so much credit.

Your credit score is a numerical version of your credit. The better your credit, the better the score. The best thing about credit scores, is that you know can tell exactly what is hurting your chances at credit. Before credit scores, we could just guess at what lenders were using to judge us. Now we know and can do something about it.

CHAPTER 9

Credit Cards

Everybody loves credit cards. They symbolize the freedom and power of credit. When someone asks you how much credit you have, they generally want to know how much your credit card limit is. "Charge it" has become a favorite catch phrase for thousands of us. Just the feeling of having thousands of dollars of purchasing power in your pocket makes you feel special.

But there is also the dark side of credit cards. When used improperly or when times get tough, the mountain of debt that piles up in a hurry can bury you. I can tell you from personal experience that it feels as if you are literally in a hole and you cannot see anything. You keep trying to climb out but the walls are so slippery that it feels like it is taking forever.

HOT TIP: The mountain of debt created by credit cards can bury you.

In this chapter, we will look at the major points of credit cards. This is not a chapter on how to use them or how to pay them off. That would have to be another book.

The Basics

There are several things you need to check whenever applying for a credit card. Depending on your credit history, some cards might not be available to you. But you need to be certain of what you are applying for so you don't get taken advantage of.

Most of these items you can determine from the information that is listed on the back of the applications. The government requires that these disclosures be provided to you so you can compare one card to another.

The Annual Fee

If you're looking for a simple, low-rate card, there's no reason to pay an annual fee. Avoid cards that charge them. Many rewards cards, such as the wildly popular air-mile credit cards and some super high-end prestige cards, charge annual fees in exchange for rewards or perks and services. Weigh these offers carefully.

The Annual Percentage Rate (APR)

The lower the interest rate, the better. Does the card come with a low introductory rate? How long does this teaser rate last? Will you be able to pay off your card balance before the teaser rate expires?

Is the APR Fixed or Variable?

Seventy percent of all credit cards have variable rates. The interest rate on a variable-rate credit card fluctuates with an index. When the index goes up or down, so does the card rate. But of course, the rate goes up a lot faster than it goes down. You didn't think they would do you any favors, did you?

Unlike variable-rate cards, the interest rate on a fixed-rate card does not fluctuate each month or each quarter. If you sign on for a card with a fixed 12.99% rate, there's a good chance you'll be paying 12.99% for quite awhile.

CREDIT SECRET: A fixed-rate card deal could change at any time. According to federal law, credit card companies only need to tell you of an increase 15 days before it takes place.

The Grace Period

A grace period is the period after a purchase is made during which interest is not charged. If payment is made in full by the end of the grace period, no interest is charged. But if it is not paid in full, interest starts at the end of the grace period.

You want the cards with the longest grace periods. The grace period should be about 25 days. That gives you a few days after receiving the statement to pay it off.

Never apply for a card with no grace period. They will start charging you interest the second you use it, even if you pay it off every month. If you carry a balance, there is no grace period, even if you have a balance of $1. The second you buy something, you start to pay interest on that purchase.

HOT TIP: Even a balance of $1 is immediately charged interest on a card with no grace period.

Penalties

Penalty rates and fees continue to go up. Make sure you find out what the charge is for paying late or going over the limit.

Going over the Limit

If you go over your spending limit, you will have to pay a big penalty fee. Over-the-limit fees of $25 and $29 are common. Most people learn about a card's over-the-limit penalty after they get charged one.

Credit card issuers have two basic choices when a customer makes a purchase that exceeds a credit limit. They can decline the transaction or approve the transaction and charge a fee. A third option, approving the transaction and automatically lifting the credit line, is reserved for the best customers.

Today's issuers are adept at targeting card offers to a customer's specific credit profile and that includes the handling of over-the-limit charges. Issuers decide what customers can go over credit limits and by how much. The last thing an issuer wants to do is decline a card purchase.

It looks like issuers will continue to charge bigger and bigger fees to customers who outgrow their credit limits, but don't let it happen to you. Here's how you can avoid over-the-limit fees:

Monitor spending closely.

Keep track of credit card purchases and stay well within your limit. Leave a big enough cushion on your card for large, unexpected expenses. Some consumer experts recommend keeping one credit card cleared for emergencies.

CREDIT SECRET: Some consumer experts recommend keeping one credit card cleared for emergencies only.

Sign up for free e-mail alerts.

Some issuers send e-mail reminders to customers who are nearing credit limits.

Make the limit your limit.

Cardholders at Capital One can request that any limit-busting purchase be declined at the point-of-sale. However, most companies refuse to provide this service.

Call ahead and get that limit raised.

If you know you're going to go over a credit limit with a purchase, call ahead and request a line increase. Issuers grant increases on a case-by-case basis. It's worth a shot and it could save you $30.

Check out cards from local banks and credit unions.

Penalty fees are much lower, typically $5 to $15, and smaller institutions are much more lenient when it comes to charging them.

The Minimum Monthly Payment

The minimum monthly payment is based on the account balance. It is about two to three percent of the account balance, or $10, whichever is greater.

Both the minimum monthly payment and the account balance are stated on the credit card statement. The monthly minimum percentage can be calculated by dividing the minimum monthly payment by the account balance.

HOT TIP: If you are paying only the minimum monthly payment it will take YEARS to pay off your balance.

In most cases, the bulk of the minimum payment goes toward interest and only a smattering goes toward principal. If your prior month's payment was late and you get hit with a $29 late fee, chances are none of the payment will go toward principal.

The following table shows how long it would take to pay off a card with a $1,000 balance if all you paid was the minimum payment every month.

$1,000 credit card balance 19 percent APR 2 percent minimum payment		
Monthly payments	**Time to pay off debt**	**Total interest you will pay**
Minimum (Starts at $20 and goes down a little each month)	22 years	$2,400

Security

One of the best things about credit cards is that it allows you to not have to carry so much cash. And if your card is stolen, the government has limited what your loss can be. Odds are if someone steals your credit cards and goes on a buying spree, it won't cost you anything. Federal law limits your liability to $50.

Most card companies will tell you that while it can cost you that $50, that fee is rarely applied.

CREDIT SECRET: Most card companies now offer some form of fraud protection. You don't need this. Do not pay for something you already have.

Report your lost or stolen cards as soon as possible for that zero-liability luxury. If you wait too long, you might not get the guaranteed protection. You should be checking your statements every month. If you see something you do not recognize, call the card company and find out more.

Getting Your Rate Lowered

If you just call your credit card company and ask them to lower the rate, they most likely will. This simple technique will save you hundreds or thousands of dollars in interest.

Check out the results of a recent national survey by the U.S. Public Interest Research Group. Fifty consumers of all credit backgrounds called credit card issuers and asked for lower rates. More than half, 56 percent, scored lower rates. How low did the rates go?

The 28 consumers who landed lower rates saw the APRs on their cards drop from an average of 16 percent to 10.47 percent.

Card companies are willing to cut interest rates, so they do not lose their customers. The competition is so fierce that it is harder to keep a customer than it is to attract a new customer. What's more, it is cheaper for them to keep you than to attract someone else to replace you.

All the consumers who participated in the PIRG survey were given the following sample script: *Hi, my name is [Your Name]. I am a good customer, but I have received several offers in the mail from other credit card companies with lower APRs. I want a lower rate on my card, or I will cancel my card and switch companies.*

Rate Lowering Game Plan

To lower your payments close to 50% of what they are now, do the following:

- Use the script. After you finish, do not say anything. Let the rep make the first offer.
- If they ask you what you want, you should respond with, "What is the best you can do?" Remember, in negotiations the first to mention a price generally misses out.
- After they give you the rate, ask, "Is that the best you can do?"
- If they say yes, ask, "Are you sure?"
- If they say yes, ask, "So if I were to tell you that that is not low enough and that I am going to transfer my balance, you still could not lower it any further?"

- Then ask what would the rate be if you transferred other balances to this card.
- Do this with all your credit cards.
- Transfer any balances that you can to cards with your new lower rates.

Chances are this will get you a really good rate.

If they don't want to play and say they can't lower the rate, ask for a supervisor. If the answer is still no, ask why. When all else fails, hang up and call again. You will probably get someone else who might be friendlier.

Not everyone who asks is going to get a lower interest rate, but long-time customers may have a better chance than newer customers. The consumers in the PIRG survey who saw their rates reduced had been with their card companies an average of four years. They were also using only 27 percent of their credit lines.

Newer customers with higher balances may have a tougher time getting their interest rates knocked down, but it's still worth a shot.

Disputing a Credit Card Charge

If you make a purchase with a credit card and there is something wrong with the merchandise, your card company may be able to help.

Credit card purchases are protected under the Fair Credit Billing Act. This law gives the consumer the right to withhold payment on poor-quality or damaged merchandise purchased with a credit card.

CREDIT SECRET: Under the Fair Credit Billing Act, you have the right to withhold payment on poor-quality or damaged merchandise purchased with a credit card.

Under the law, you do need to make a real effort at resolving the dispute with the merchant before you can ask your issuer to stop a credit card payment. There are, however, a few other catches.

The sale must be for more than $50 and must have taken place in your home state or within 100 miles of your home address. Few issuers enforce the $50 or 100-mile rule on purchases, but all are free to do so.

Most card companies will issue a temporary credit to a customer's account when a purchase is in dispute. The card company then contacts the merchant. If they agree with the customer, the refund stands. If they side with the merchant, the customer must pay for the item, plus any accrued finance charges.

Some card companies may be less generous when a big-ticket item is in dispute or if you made the purchase while traveling overseas. It all depends on the card company and how much they value you as a customer. They can point to the limits spelled out in the Fair Credit Billing Act whenever they want to.

In your letter, be sure to include your credit card account number, the closing date of the bill on which the disputed charge appears, a description of the disputed item and why you're withholding payment. Enclose a copy of your complaint letter to the merchant and any other documentation you may have in support of your position.

Send your letter by certified mail, return receipt requested, to the credit card company at the address for "billing inquiries," not to the address for payments.

A credit card company cannot charge you finance charges on a disputed charge, but you will still be charged interest on any other purchases you may have made. Be sure to include a payment for these purchases with your letter.

Don't delay in the mailing of your dispute letter, especially if it includes a payment. Under the Fair Credit Billing Act, an issuer can take as many as five days to credit a payment not sent to the payment address.

To dispute a bill, it's best to move quickly. You'll want to inform your card issuer of the disputed charge before it's due for payment. You can't withhold a payment once a bill is paid.

Cash Advances

Unless you are thousands of miles from home and need something for which they will only accept cash, never use your credit cards for cash advances. Cash advances are when you use an ATM to get money from a credit card or when you use the convenience checks that come in the mail. Your credit card is not a debit card.

CREDIT SECRET: If you can help it, never use your credit cards for cash advances.

Here is why:

- Cash advances carry an upfront fee of 2–4% of the amount advanced.
- They have a higher interest rate than regular card charges.
- They carry no grace period; interest charges begin to mount as soon as the money spits out of the ATM.
- Many issuers also require you to pay down the balances for purchases before you pay down the higher-interest cash advance balance.

The fees and charges applied to cash advances are not hidden fees. By law, card issuers are required to disclose information about fees and charges associated with all of their services. This information is typically displayed on the back of the solicitation form and on the monthly statements.

Let's see what you pay when you withdraw $20 from your credit card at an ATM.

First, the ATM will charge you around $1.50. Second, the card company will charge you either a minimum fee or a percentage. In this case, let's say 5%, so that is $1. Third, the interest starts as soon as you get the money and the rate is an amazing 22%. So, by the time you get your statement 30 days later, you owe 37 cents. Doesn't sound like much, but you didn't take out much and that is if you don't have an existing balance. Fourth, by the time your payment reaches the company, you owe more interest, another 25 cents.

So in total, your $20 cash advance costs you $23.12. You paid 13% more than you borrowed! Imagine getting a 13% per month return on your investments. You would be rich in months.

How many cards should you have?

Most people only need 3–4 cards. I have seen many people with over 20 cards. Their wallets are so big that they don't fit in their pockets.

You can have as many as you are comfortable with. The more you have, however, the more risk is involved, not only if they get stolen, but also if you miss a payment as a result of the bill getting misplaced or never arriving. If you have too many, you won't be able to keep track of all of them.

As far as your credit score is concerned, you can get penalized for having too few cards and too many. At least three and not more than ten seems to be a good range. Of course, you want your limits to be as high as possible and your balances to be as low as possible.

Credit and Debit Card Blocking

Have you ever been told you were over your credit card limit, or had your debit card declined, even though you knew you had available credit, or money in your bank account? If this happened shortly after you stayed in a hotel or rented a car, the problem could have been card "blocking."

When you use a credit or debit card to check into a hotel or rent a car, the clerk usually contacts the company that issued your card to give an estimated total. If the transaction is approved, your available credit (credit card) or the balance in your bank account (debit card) is reduced by this amount. That's a "block." Some companies also call this placing a "hold" on those amounts.

Here's how it works. Suppose you use a credit or debit card when you check into a $100-a-night hotel for five nights. At least $500 would likely be blocked. In addition, hotels and rental car companies often add anticipated charges for "incidentals" like food, beverages, or gasoline to the blocked amount. These incidental amounts can vary widely among merchants.

If you pay your bill with the same card you used when you checked in, the final charge on your credit card, or final amount on your debit card, probably will replace the block in a day or two. However, if you pay your bill with a different card, or with cash or a check, the company that issued the card you used at check-in might hold the block for up to 15 days after you've checked out. That's because they weren't notified of the final payment and didn't know you paid another way.

Why Blocking Can Be a Problem

Blocking is used to make sure you don't exceed your credit line (credit card) or overdraw your bank account (debit card) before checking out of a hotel or returning a rental car, leaving the merchant unpaid. Blocking is sometimes also used by restaurants for anticipated sizeable bills (like large groups at dinner or a party), by companies cleaning your home and other businesses to ensure credit or account money will be available to complete payment.

If you're nowhere near your credit limit or have a low balance in your bank account, blocking probably won't be a problem. But if you're reaching that point, be careful. Not only can it be embarrassing to have your card declined, it also can be inconvenient, especially if you have an emergency purchase and insufficient credit or money in your bank account. On debit cards, depending on the balance in your bank account, blocking could lead to charges for insufficient funds while the block remains in place.

How to Avoid Blocking

To avoid the aggravation that blocking can cause, follow these tips:

- When you check into a hotel or rent a car—or if a restaurant or other business asks for your card in advance of service—ask if the company is "blocking," how much will be blocked, how the amount is determined, and how long the block remains in place.
- Consider paying hotel, motel, rental car, or other "blocked" bills with the same credit or debit card you used at the beginning of the transaction. Ask the clerk when the prior block will be removed.
- If you pay with a different card, by cash, or by check, remind the clerk you're using a different form of payment and ask them to remove the prior block promptly.
- Ask your current debit card issuer if they permit blocks, for how long, and from what types of merchants. If they do, you may want to consider getting an overdraft line of credit from your bank. Ask about a plan that always automatically covers the overdraft and does not involve a separate bank decision on whether or not to pay it each time. Although you might incur some interest on this plan if you don't pay off the amount fairly quickly, you would not have an overdraft that is not paid. Ask your bank if they offer an overdraft line of credit, how it would work, and how much it costs.

In addition, if you are considering a credit or debit card, shop around. When comparing credit and debit card offers, ask issuers if they permit blocks, for how long, and from what types of merchants. You may want to consider an issuer that uses shorter blocks.

Credit Card Loss Protection Offers: They're the Real Steal

"I got a call from a woman who said I need credit card loss protection insurance. I thought there was a law that limited my liability to $50 for unauthorized charges. But she said the law had changed and that now, people are liable for all unauthorized charges on their account. Is that true?"

Don't buy the pitch—and don't buy the "loss protection" insurance. Telephone scam artists are lying to get people to buy worthless credit card loss protection and insurance programs. If you didn't authorize a charge, don't pay it. Follow your credit card issuer's procedures for disputing charges you haven't authorized. According to the FTC, your liability for unauthorized charges is limited to $50.

The FTC says worthless credit card loss protection offers are popular among fraudulent promoters who are trying to exploit consumers' uncertainty. As a result, the agency is cautioning consumers to avoid doing business with callers who claim that:

- You're liable for more than $50 in unauthorized charges on your credit card account;
- You need credit card loss protection because computer hackers can access your credit card number and charge thousands of dollars to your account;
- A computer bug could make it easy for thieves to place unauthorized charges on your credit card account; and
- They're from "the security department" and want to activate the protection feature on your credit card.

The FTC advises consumers not to give out personal information—including their credit card or bank account numbers—over the phone or online unless they are familiar with the business that's asking for it. Scam artists can use your personal information to commit fraud, such as identity theft. That's where someone uses some piece of your personal information, such as your credit card account number, Social Security number, mother's maiden name, or birth date, without your knowledge or permission to commit fraud or theft. An all-too-common example is when an identity thief uses your personal information to open a credit card account in your name.

Not only do you have to beware of scam artists, but the banks themselves have gotten into the act big time. Their constant goal is to get as much money from you as possible. And one way is to offer these seemingly valuable services for a small fee. Like the Credit Protector Program at Citibank. This program says it will cover charges if your card is stolen. And it will pay your monthly minimum payment if you get sick and cannot work.

They try to entice you by saying there is only a charge if you carry a balance. But most people do not even need these services, and those that do use them, find they paid a lot more then what they got in return. When it got time to collect on this "insurance" the fine print made collecting anything almost impossible.

I get numerous e-mails from my website and from newsletter subscribers that complain about how they were tricked into signing up for this type of service. Most credit card companies have them. But beware. You don't need it.

Hint: A favorite trick of the banks is to send you a real check for a small amount. If you deposit the check, you automatically sign up for their program. Remember — there's no such thing as a free lunch!

A note about store credit cards:

Store credit cards, such as Sears, now carry in the fine print a new method of collection in case you stop paying. According to the card agreement, you agree that any merchandise bought using that card becomes collateral. So if you do not pay, Sears legally can send people to your house to search for the things you bought on that card.

Normally they would not do this, because they are not in the business of selling used goods, but they will and DO use it as a threat to get people to pay them. They have also gone as far as calling relatives of deceased people and using this threat to get payment for the deceased's account.

CHAPTER 10

Mortgages

As the owner of a mortgage company, I can honestly tell you that anyone can be approved for a mortgage regardless of their credit, provided that they are ready to pay for it. Bad credit does not have to be a barrier to owning a home, but it sure can make it more costly.

CREDIT SECRET: Bad credit need not be a barrier to owning your own home.

When you apply for a mortgage, the lender will first check your credit to see what grade of loan you will qualify for. It is this grade that determines your interest rate. Note that while credit is not the only factor that determines the rate, it *is* the main factor. Other factors include length of employment and income. The different grades are A, B, C and D. A is the best, followed by the rest. These grades also depend on the lender. Some lenders, such as banks, don't even have grades. You either meet their requirements or you don't. Depending on the lender, there are also pluses and minuses such as A+, A-, B+, B-, etc.

Credit scores also play a huge role in determining if you qualify for a loan and what grade you get.

The best option for someone with bad credit is to see a good mortgage broker. Mortgage brokers work with several different lenders, including banks, private investors, hard equity lenders, mortgage bankers, pension funds and insurance companies. The better the mortgage company you have, the better terms they will be able to get you. They have the ability to shop your application around to several lenders to get you the best rate, unlike banks which only have a couple of loan programs. Lenders also vary greatly. You might qualify for an A mortgage with one lender and a C with another.

Your recent credit history is the most important when applying for a loan. Any recent negative items will definitely hurt, no matter how large or small the amount. By recent, I mean within the past 12 months. A common myth that goes around is that to qualify for a mortgage you must first pay off all your negative outstanding debts. Some lenders require this, others do not.

Unpaid tax liens or judgments present a major obstacle in receiving your loan. A bankruptcy declared within the past one or two years will also be a major problem. The more negative accounts with unpaid balances you have, the worse your chance of qualifying. It is in your best interest to pay off some of these accounts prior to applying for the mortgage. Those accounts could either cause your application to be rejected or cause your interest rate to be higher than it need be. Keep in mind that even a little difference in the rate could cost you thousands of dollars in interest.

CREDIT SECRET: Unpaid tax liens or judgments present a major obstacle when applying for a mortgage.

Another option you have (in a refinancing situation) is to use your loan money to pay off your accounts. Some lenders might even require this. The lender, at closing, will automatically withhold the amount you owe and pay your debts for you.

If you go to negotiate with your creditors to get your debts paid off before applying for a mortgage, do not tell your debtors why you are paying them off. Once they realize you are applying for a loan, they will have the upper-hand and will not likely deal with you. Therefore, it is best for you to negotiate with your creditors yourself to pay off your debts before applying for the loan.

CREDIT SECRET: It is best to pay off your debts before applying for a mortgage.

If you contact them after you apply for the loan, there will be an inquiry from the mortgage company on your credit report and it will tip them off. One of the best weapons collection agencies have is to wait to collect the debt until the consumer wants to buy a house. At that time, the agency is most likely to collect the full amount they are asking and therefore will not negotiate. The most important weapon you have against them is that only you know what your current situation is. Don't give them the upper hand.

The amount of late payments and the length of their lateness are also important to lenders. A 30-day late payment is not as bad as a 90-date late payment. And of course ten late payments are worse than one or two. One item that can cause you to be rejected outright is late payment on your current mortgage. The lender is mostly interested in getting his money back with interest. If he sees that you are not even paying your current mortgage on time, what insurance does he have that you will pay him on time? None.

A foreclosure is the ultimate black mark when applying for a loan, but don't get discouraged. Remember, in this country anything is possible. You can work your way around any negative marks on your credit report, but in order to do so you will definitely need a good mortgage broker.

The mortgage broker gets paid by either you, the lender, or both, in the form of points. Every point that a lender receives is worth 1% of the loan amount and each point can either raise or lower your interest rate. The worse your credit, the more work will be involved in qualifying you, so the more points the broker will charge. Ask your broker exactly how much he is getting. First and foremost, it is the broker's job to find which lender is best for you, and then to help you qualify with that lender.

Your job is to find the best broker. There is a lot of money made in mortgages and that's why there are thousands of mortgage companies throughout the country. And they all seem to guarantee the lowest rates. Unfortunately, most mortgage company employees are untrained and have no idea what they are doing. Therefore, it is extremely important that you find a good mortgage broker who knows how to best handle your case. By shopping around, you will no doubt be offered various interest rates. You will also learn what the industry averages are for certain required fees, such as the credit report ($55–60), the appraisal ($250–300) and the processing fees (varies). All of the fees can be negotiated. It doesn't hurt to ask the mortgage company to waive a few or all of the fees.

More and more lenders are requiring at least one credit score on all applications. Each of the three major bureaus has at least one credit (risk) scoring system. I cover the credit score in depth in another chapter, but your score could be the difference between qualifying for an A loan or a B loan. The higher your score, the better off you are.

HOT TIP: The reporting agency cannot change anything in your credit report that each of the three main bureaus have on you. You will need to file a dispute to do that.

Today's mortgage application is taken differently than in the past. Mortgage brokers and lender today use the Internet and a new technology to work faster and more efficiently. There is less need for hundreds of documents. And loans can be approved in minutes instead of weeks.

The credit process for mortgages has changed as well. Factuals are no longer done. Today's mortgage company will pull a three-file, merged credit report. This is a simple report of all three bureaus merged together into one. The mortgage broker will sit down at his computer, go to the credit reporting agency's website, pull your reports, and have it print out in a couple minutes. The report will be saved on his hard drive and forwarded to the lender along with your application. If there is anything incorrect on your report, the credit reporting agency will be asked to investigate. Employment and other verifications are no longer done by the credit reporting agency. They are done by your lender directly.

But the largest shift in the mortgage business has been the introduction of credit scores. As early as 1995, credit scores came on the scene. I remember the first mortgage company asking for a credit score on a report. We knew what it was, but we had to make changes to our computer software so we could print the credit score onto the reports.

Since then, credit scores have become the number one factor in determining your interest rate. As I said before, you can be approved for a mortgage even if your credit isn't good, but you will pay a lot more in interest and fees. So the better your score, the lower your monthly payment, the less you pay in interest, the less you have to put as a down payment, and the more you can borrow.

You now know how bad credit affects your mortgage application, but how do you improve your application in the lender's eyes, in such a way that they don't view you as a credit risk?

Well, one way, which we already discussed, is to pay off your delinquent accounts. After you've paid all you can, it's time to get creative. No matter how bad your credit report is, several companies still extend credit to you every day. Do you pay your electricity bill every day? Do you pay for each phone call before you make it? Do you send the cable company a check every day? Of course not! These companies bill you at the end of the month. That, my friend, is credit. Best of all, you can use this credit to help you get your mortgage.

In order to add these accounts to your Factual or tri-merged report, you will need a credit reference letter from each of these companies. Just call them up and ask for one. Give these letters to your mortgage company so the credit reporting agency can add them to your credit report.

CREDIT SECRET: Call up your utility companies and ask them for a reference, which can then be added to your credit report.

These good accounts will show that you have been paying promptly in the last year or so. These accounts can balance out the negative accounts. Any other accounts that you paid in installments that do not appear on your credit report can also be added. Examples are your car insurance, your jewelry or furniture purchases, or your used car purchase.

Some more tips on getting the best mortgage deal:

- Visit at least three different banks and brokers to compare rates and service.
- According to the National Association of Realtors, most people move in 5–7 years. When getting a mortgage, do not "buydown" the rate. That is, do not pay additional money to get a lower interest rate than you are getting. This almost never ends up working in the homeowner's favor.
- Have your lender "lock" your rate, so that they cannot increase it later. The most notorious scheme in the industry is to quote a very cheap rate that no one else can even match, and then at the closing table inform the borrowers that the rate went up several percentage points.
- Get your credit in shape before you visit the mortgage company.
- Get pre-approved for a loan before looking for homes. This gives you an idea of how much home you qualify for and eliminates worries about getting the loan after you fall in love with a house.
- Get your own insurance from your own agent. And here I am talking about Homeowner's Insurance. This is the policy that covers your house, belongings and liability.
- If you can, put 20 percent down so you do not have to have Mortgage Insurance. This is a policy for the bank—not for you. Or you can get a first and second loan together to keep your down payment low. A 80/15/5 is a loan where you have a 80% first mortgage, 15% second, and 5% down payment. This will keep you from paying Mortgage Insurance.
- See if you qualify for an FHA loan. FHA loans are easier to get for people with lower income, bad credit and less money down. The rates are also very good.

- When working with a mortgage broker, if you have negative information on your credit that you can prove is a mistake, the broker might be able to get that information off your report. Make sure to give him any documents you have and insist that he deliver those to the credit reporting agency and have them verify the accounts.

CREDIT SECRET: When applying for a mortgage, do not "buydown" the rate.

PERSONAL STORY: In 2002, I bought a house in pre-foreclosure from a man who had recently divorced. His finances were shot, and he couldn't afford the mortgage by himself. So instead of letting the bank have it, he gave it to me. For free. I mention this not to brag, but to show that getting a house for free is possible—if you know where to look. Actually it wasn't totally free. I had to pay the bank around $5000 to stop the foreclosure. And I paid about $4000 to fix up the house, so I could resell it.

Unknown to me when I bought the house, it was in a very hot neighborhood. We used to get at least eight calls a day from people interested in buying it, and all we had was a sign in the yard. But everyone thought I was asking too much. I was. I was asking $10,000 more than it was worth. But I like to think that I know what I am doing, and one day a woman called me and wanted to buy.

So I sent her and her husband to my mortgage company to get a loan. That's when the bad news came. Their credit was bad. We could get them a loan, but it was at 10% (the best rate available to people with perfect credit at the time was 7%).

And they only had $5000. That was $13,000 less than they needed for the down payment and closing costs.

But they had really fallen in love with the house and didn't want to negotiate on the price, so I decided to lease-option them the house. I would rent them the house for 12 months at $1300 a month. They would give me the $5000 as a non-refundable deposit. And I would let them buy the house at the set price of $130,000 anytime within those twelve months. But if they didn't, or couldn't buy in 12 months, they would have to move out and lose the $5000. They agreed.

Eleven months later, the woman called me, ready to get her loan. So we went back to my mortgage company. While her credit had improved some, she was still $10,000 short of what she needed.

So I did the only thing my conscious would let me do. Because I didn't want to keep her $5,000, and I didn't want to have to go through the selling process again, I gave her a second mortgage for the $10,000 at 12% for 5 years. They had always paid the rent on time and were good people. So I took a risk. They closed on the house and even invited me to dinner.

If You Still Cannot Get A Loan

There are three main criteria for getting a loan:

- credit
- income
- down payment

If you have two of the three you can get a mortgage. If you have only one, or none, you are going to have a hard time buying a house. But there is hope.

If you read the last story, I highlighted three different techniques anyone with lousy credit can use to buy a house with not much down.

The first technique was the way I bought the house. In real estate circles, it is called subject-to. What I did was pay the bank to make the payments current. Then have the seller sign the deed to my company. That made my company the legal owner of the house, and it kept the loan in the seller's name. I did not need any money to give to the seller, nor did anyone check my credit or income. And there was no title or escrow company in the middle and no extra fees to pay. We just sat at the kitchen table and signed the papers. The bank never even knew the house had been sold.

The second method is the lease option. This is where you do not have enough down payment or need more time to fix your credit, but you have already found the house you wish to buy. And some sellers will allow a portion of the rent you pay every month to go toward the down payment. So if your rent is $1200, the seller might let $200 go toward the down payment. So after one year, the seller will say that you already gave him $2400 in cash as down payment.

The third option is seller financing. If the seller is desperate enough, he might agree to loan you some of the money if you cannot get enough of a loan from the bank. If you have bad credit, normally the bank will want at least 10% down. But if you have less, ask the seller to lend you some. All you have to do is ask. In commercial deals, this happens all the time.

These are only short explanations of the methods I used. There are many, many other creative financing techniques you can use. Creative financing is a topic for another book. But if you are interested hop on down to your local library and check out all the "No Down Payment" and real estate investment books you can find. I have to warn you though, many of the techniques will be outdated and won't work today, but there are still many good ideas in those books.

If you liked the above story, the next one will blow you away.

PERSONAL STORY: In 2001, I had bought a house through a lease option. This one was also from a divorced man. After a couple weeks of having it for up sale, I got a buyer. We negotiated a little and came to an agreement. This man wanted to use his own mortgage company, which had already approved him for a loan.

But get this: He had declared bankruptcy less than 1 year ago, was set to retire from his job (where he had worked for 27 years) in three years, and had very little money for the down payment. I couldn't believe it when he told me he was already approved for a loan. Luckily for him, he qualified for a VA loan, with 0% down payment, and where they don't care about your credit.

The only problem was that he didn't have enough for the closing costs. So he asked me to pay for them. I didn't want to give away over $3000, and plus, I had closing costs of my own to pay. So we did the following. We raised the price of the house $3000, I offered to pay $3000 in closing costs, and he increased the loan amount $3000 to cover it. So basically he got the VA to finance his closing costs as well!

That's a simple trick you might try.

Private Mortgage Insurance

If you put less than 20 percent down on a home mortgage, lenders will require you to have Private Mortgage Insurance (PMI). This PMI protects the lender if you default on the loan. This policy does not cover you for anything. You are essentially paying money to protect the lender. If you do not pay your mortgage and the bank forecloses in most cases, the bank can only recover 80% of the value of the house. Even if there is some equity, there are costs involved such as legal fees, court costs, rehabbing the house and selling expense. So if you owe more than 80% of the value of the house, and the bank has to foreclose on it, the bank would lose money. And banks hate losing money, so they have you pay for insurance, which will pay them for any money that they lose by foreclosing on you.

Let's say you owe them $90,000 on a $100,000 house. After the foreclosure, if they can sell the house for $80,000, you still owe them $10,000. They can still come after you for this $10,000 and get a deficiency judgment. But the PMI will pay them the $10,000, so they might not come after you for it.

Once your mortgage balance is lower than 80%, either because you paid it down, or the value of your house went up, you can have this PMI stopped. Until then, the lender will add the cost of the PMI to your mortgage payment.

The Homeowners Protection Act of 1998—which became effective in 1999—establishes rules for automatic termination and borrower cancellation of PMI on home mortgages. These protections apply to certain home mortgages signed on, or after, July 29, 1999 for the purchase, initial construction or refinance of a single-family home. These protections ***do not*** apply to government-insured FHA or VA loans or to loans with lender-paid PMI. If you get an FHA or VA loan, you will be paying PMI for the life of the loan.

For home mortgages signed *on or after* July 29, 1999, your PMI must—with certain exceptions—be terminated automatically when you reach 22 percent equity in your home, based on the original property value, if your mortgage payments are current. Your PMI also can be canceled, when you request—with certain exceptions—when you reach 20 percent equity in your home based on the original property value, if your mortgage payments are current.

One exception is if your loan is "high-risk." Another is if you have not been current on your payments within the year prior to the time for termination or cancellation. A third is if you have other liens on your property. For these loans, your PMI may continue. Ask your lender or mortgage servicer (a company that collects your payments) for more information about these requirements.

If you signed your mortgage *before* July 29, 1999, you can ask to have the PMI canceled once you exceed 20 percent equity in your home. But federal law does not require your lender or mortgage servicer to cancel the insurance.

On a $100,000 loan with 10 percent down ($10,000), PMI might cost you $40 a month. If you can cancel the PMI, you can save $480 a year and many thousands of dollars over the loan. Check your annual escrow account statement or call your lender to find out exactly how much PMI is costing you each year.

Additional Provisions in the Law

- New borrowers covered by the law must be told—at closing and once a year—about PMI termination and cancellation.
- Mortgage servicers must provide a telephone number for all their mortgage borrowers to call for information about termination and cancellation of PMI.
- Even though the law's termination and cancellation rights do not cover loans that were signed before July 29, 1999, or loans with lender-paid PMI signed on any date, lenders or mortgage servicers must tell borrowers about the termination or cancellation rights they may otherwise have under those loans (such as rights established by the contract or state law).

Next Steps

Some states may have laws that apply to early termination or cancellation of PMI, even if you signed your mortgage before July 29, 1999. Call your state consumer protection agency for more information about your state's rules. Fannie Mae and Freddie Mac, which buy home mortgages from lenders, also may have guidelines affecting termination or cancellation of PMI on home mortgages signed before July 29, 1999. Check with your lender or mortgage servicer, or call Fannie Mae or Freddie Mac, for more information.

Contact your lender or mortgage servicer to learn whether you're paying PMI. If you are, ask how and when it can be terminated or canceled.

CHAPTER 11

Divorce

Divorce can be a trying time for the entire family. There are so many different things to keep track of and fight over that credit might be overlooked. The couple's finances add another element to consider when getting divorced. In order to make a clean break, the finances need to be taken care of very carefully. Divorce attorneys are not financial experts. They know how to fill out the paperwork and not much else. Don't expect credible advice from your attorney on how to handle your finances and credit responsibilities.

Joint accounts can be especially messy if not taken care of properly. A joint account is a legal contract between you, your spouse and your creditor. Both of you are responsible for all charges on the account. The divorce decree is also a legally binding contract, but it does NOT cancel any prior contracts between you and your creditors. Both you and your spouse are still responsible for your debts, no matter what the divorce decree says. The creditors can and will come after both of you for payment. Many credit files have been ruined by ex-spouses who did not pay the bills. Don't let this happen to you.

CREDIT SECRET: A divorce decree does NOT cancel any prior contracts between you and your creditors.

When divorcing, contact all your creditors and cancel all your joint accounts. Your creditors might even open new individual accounts for you and transfer the balances to these new accounts. Do what you need to do to protect your credit, perhaps by taking out a personal loan, or putting the cards where neither of you can get at them. If not, make sure the payments are being made every billing statement, or have your attorney do this for you.

In most states, if you are married you are responsible for:

- Joint accounts
- Family necessities such as food shelter and clothing
- Your children's education

Both spouses are also responsible for these three items until the divorce is finalized. A spouse is not responsible for any debts run up by the mate before marriage or after divorce.

HOT TIP: You are not responsible for any debts run up by your spouse prior to your marriage.

If you are heading for divorce, take the following steps:

1. Before filing for divorce, close all joint accounts and try to get them switched to personal accounts with only one person responsible. If that is not possible, try paying the account off. At least if the account is closed, neither spouse can run up the bill after the divorce.
2. Check each spouse's credit and establish it before the divorce. Apply for your own cards and loans before the divorce so you can list both spouses' income on the application.

After Divorce

So what do you do if you are already divorced and your ex has screwed up your credit? You will still be responsible for repayment. There is not much you can do to get out of that and most creditors will not forgive you.

If your spouse's negative accounts are hurting your credit rating, you do have some options. The ECOA Regulation B Section 202.6(b)(6) says: "To the extent that a creditor considers credit history in evaluating the creditworthiness of …applicants… a creditor shall consider …(ii) on the applicants request, any information the applicant may present that tends to indicate that the credit history being considered by the creditor does not accurately reflect that applicant's creditworthiness…"

This means that legally a potential creditor must look at any evidence that shows that your credit report does not represent your financial qualifications. There is really no way to make sure the creditors do this, but it may help. Some items you could show to help establish your creditworthiness would be your credit history before marriage or the divorce, and proof that the derogatory accounts belong to your spouse as per the divorce decree. This will help when applying for a mortgage. Make sure you turn in a copy of the decree to your loan officer.

Community Property States

In community property states (Arizona, California, Idaho, Louisiana, Nevada, New Mexico, Texas, Washington and Wisconsin), the rules are a bit different. In those states, all property acquired during the marriage and any debts incurred while married belong to both partners jointly.

- Both spouses are responsible for all debts unless the creditor is holding only one spouse responsible for repayment.

- Spouses are not responsible for debts before or after marriage.
- Separate property is only that which is owned before marriage or received during marriage by only one spouse, by gift or inheritance.
- Community property also includes all income earned by both partners during the marriage, except for income earned on property that was acquired before marriage, such as income producing property or interest payments on a loan.

HOT TIP: In community property states, all property acquired and any debts incurred during the marriage belong to both partners jointly.

If your ex has messed up your credit after divorce, there is not much you can do unless you want to pay off those accounts. If you wait seven years, however, those accounts will automatically come off your credit report. In the meantime, continue to pay your bills on time and strengthen your credit. Eventually your positive efforts will outweigh the negative.

CHAPTER 12

Bankruptcy

Sometimes, when the debts and payments get so high that they cannot be made, there is no other alternative than to declare bankruptcy. Most people think that bankruptcy is going to court and having all your bills miraculously wiped away. Anyone who has been through one can tell you it is not as easy as people make it out to be. It can be expensive, time-consuming, a huge hassle and a real credit killer. If you think your credit is bad before bankruptcy, it is ten times worse afterwards.

Millions of Americans have filed for bankruptcy, often using the process as an "alternative." How wrong. Filing for bankruptcy is the last resort to your financial woes, not a choice. Bankruptcy is a tool to be used when there is no going back…a fail-safe.

There are two main types of bankruptcies for individuals, Chapter 7 and Chapter 13. Chapter 7 gets rid of all debts (except some taxes and maybe alimony payments); Chapter 13 allows you, when in debt and with a steady income, to pay off your bills over a 36- to 60-month period.

HOT TIP: There are two individual types of bankruptcies: Chapter 7 and Chapter 13.

Chapter 13 lets you get your financial house in order. You must repay your debts by following a set plan that you suggest to a Trustee, who is appointed by the court. The Trustee then distributes the money to your creditors.

Here's how bankruptcies work. When you file either Chapter 7 or Chapter 13, you are issued a restraining order by the court, which will protect you from all further proceedings against you until all previous debts are cleared. This is called an automatic stay and stops all creditors, for a short time, from taking any further action against you. Your state laws determine how long the stay will be in effect. For example, in Texas, declaring Chapter 7 will not stop a foreclosure action that has already been filed. The restraining order includes protection against such items as wage garnishment, creditor harassment and foreclosures without a court order.

Chapter 7 is for people who have few or no secured debts. Credit card debt is unsecured debt, and most people who file Chapter 7 owe only credit card debt. By declaring Chapter 7, those unsecured debts are forgiven. Chapter 7 debtors can sign a "reaffirmation agreement" that allows them to keep paying some types of secured debt, such as auto loans.

Chapter 13 is for people with substantial secured debt. That means they have home mortgages or car loans. Under Chapter 13, homeowners can stay in their houses while repaying their debts, under a court-supervised spending plan that lasts three to five years. Regardless of chapter, a debtor is almost always required to pay federal taxes and student-loan debt.

HOT TIP: The bright side to filing for bankruptcy is immediate relief. The dark side is a black mark that remains on your credit record, haunting you for 10 years.

Chapter 7

Commonly known as liquidation, this form of bankruptcy basically allows filers to give up assets in exchange for discharge of their debts. This is frequently the option for people who have few or no assets, little or no income, and a lot of debt. You use Chapter 7 when there is no way you will ever be able to pay off your unsecured debts, i.e., credit cards, medical bills, personal loans, etc. The court lets you keep homesteaded property, most retirement plans and certain other personal items. This is called exempt property, and each state's exemptions are a little different.

Whatever is left over is called non-exempt property and will be sold. The proceeds will be used to pay creditors in accordance with state law. When the proceedings are over, any debts that haven't been paid are discharged, or forgiven, and except for the black mark on your credit report, you start fresh.

Bankruptcy stops most garnishments, although it depends on why you're being garnished. What you will be allowed to keep will depend largely on your state laws. Some states allow you to keep all of the equity in your home, while others exempt a certain amount. In some places, individuals may keep their household goods. Some states, like Virginia, allow filers to keep wedding and engagement rings.

Chapter 7 usually takes three to five months from the date of filing to the final discharge. You can file only once in six years.

There are some unsecured debts that are never—or hardly ever—dischargeable, including overdue child support and alimony payments, student loans, taxes, and debts from criminal behavior. If these are your debts, Chapter 7 probably isn't going to help you.

This option will also be more damaging to your credit rating than a Chapter 13 filing, according to John Ulzheimer, a solutions delivery consultant with Fair, Isaac & Co., the company that pioneered credit scoring and created the model for the FICO score. The impact will vary depending on how recently the bankruptcy occurred and how many debts were discharged. "The more accounts, the more impact," says Ulzheimer. As the bankruptcy gets older, even though it remains on the report, the "impact will diminish," says Ulzheimer.

Chapter 13

This is the reorganization chapter. You generally file for protection under Chapter 13 when you have fallen hopelessly behind in paying your secured debt, such as your mortgage and car payments. Some of your debts will be reduced, and past due amounts will be reorganized, so they can be paid over a three- to five-year period. The court will not let you do this unless you have enough income to make payments on the reorganized debt and, at the same time, can keep current on your regular monthly bills.

If you do not live in a community property state and one spouse files bankruptcy, the other spouse will not be responsible if they did not authorize the purchases that led to the debt.

Whether you're up to your neck in loans, out of work, or stretching one small paycheck to meet ever-growing obligations, nearly everyone occasionally flirts with the idea of ditching their debt. But the reality of bankruptcy is that it's a complicated legal procedure that will severely damage your credit rating. Many states have their own bankruptcy regulations, which can make a big difference in what property you're allowed to keep.

Since bankruptcy is a court-monitored activity, the bankruptcy trustee, your creditors, and a judge will also be involved.

Chapter 13 differentiates between three types of debt:

- Priority debts, which often include some taxes and child support, have to be paid in full. In addition, individuals may be liable for interest that accrues on priority debts after the bankruptcy is filed.
- Secured debts, which are debts secured with some form of collateral, must be paid up to the full value with interest over the life of the plan.
- Unsecured debts, like credit cards, typically receive just a percentage of the total due. The amount will vary depending on the individual's disposable income, amount of the original debt and how many creditors are waiting in line.

Chapter 13 also allows filers to eliminate some tax liabilities, including those that result from late filing, not filing, and fraud. But if the tax debt is relatively recent, the debt has to be paid in full.

The repayment plan must be approved by the bankruptcy court and both the trustee and the creditors are allowed to object. Sometimes individuals file for Chapter 13 only to find out they must convert it to a Chapter 7. Also, there are monetary limits to the amount of debt you can have in a Chapter 13.

If the plan passes muster with the court, then all disposable income is given to the trustee, who keeps a percentage as a fee and parcels out the rest to the creditors in accordance with the plan. There is no time limit for filing a second Chapter 13, but a creditor could ask to have serial attempts dismissed as "bad-faith filings."

You can use Chapter 13 to buy some time if creditors are threatening you. If you are about to be foreclosed on, you can file for Chapter 13 then sell your house and not have to go through with the bankruptcy.

Chapter 13 requires a lot of discipline. For the entire repayment period (3 to 5 years), you have to live under the strict budget that you created and the court agreed to. You cannot spend money on anything that the court thinks is nonessential.

CREDIT SECRET: Most people do not even finish their repayment periods. Only 35% of all debtors complete their plan.

Chapter 13 should be used instead of Chapter 7 in the following cases:

- You are behind on your mortgage or car loan.
- You have a tax debt.
- You really want to repay your debts.
- You want help reorganizing but want to leave the Chapter 7 route open for later use.
- You are a family farmer.
- You have a lot of valuable nonexempt property, such as collections (stamps, dolls, coins, etc.), family heirlooms, investments, a second car or home.
- You already declared Chapter 7 within the past 6 years.
- You have a co-borrower on your debt.

Bankruptcy Abuse Prevention and Consumer Protection Act of 2005

After failing seven times, the lobbing efforts of banks and credit cards companies finally got what they wanted: a law to make it harder for people to declare bankruptcy. The Bankruptcy Abuse Prevention and Consumer Protection Act of 2005 was signed into law by President Bush on April 20, 2005.

This new law is the largest overhaul of the bankruptcy code since it was created in 1978. The Act was written to help reduce the filing of bankruptcies and "the absence of effective oversight" in the system.

The main changes to the bill for consumers is the means test, and credit counseling requirement.

Means Test

The most influential part of the new law is the implantation of a mean test to see if an individual can file for bankruptcy and which chapter he can file for. Under the test, a low income debtor would be eligible for Chapter 7 if the amount of his income minus allowed expenses is less than $100 per month. At the high end, the debtor would not be eligible is the monthly net income is $166.67 a month or higher. Only debtors whose net monthly income exceeds their state's median income would be subject to the means test. Also, to qualify for Chapter 7, the debtor must not be able to pay more than 25% of all nonpriority unsecured claims if income less expenses multiplied by 60 is between $6,000 and $10,000.

Confused? Here's an example to help clarify.

Our debtor, Jay, after deducting all allowable expenses from his monthly income, has more left over that the median amount of his state. Let's say he has $100 net monthly income. He passes the first test because his net income is lower than $166.67. But he has $15,000 of unsecured non priority debt. Twenty-five percent of that is $3,750. If Jay paid $100 a month for 5 years he could pay $6,000. This makes Jay ineligible to Chapter 7. If Jay owed $25,000 he would qualify because 25% of $25,000 is $6,250, and that is more than the $6,000 Jay would have in five years.

The allowable expenses are specified by IRS standards, and are too complicated to get into here.

The Act also requires all attorneys to perform the means test on their clients before filing. If the attorney calculates wrongly, he is subject to civil penalties. What this means is that many attorneys will not take the risk and will not advise Chapter 7 filing. They will watch out for themselves instead of you.

Credit Counseling

The Act requires that debtors provide a certificate of credit counseling and repayment plan from an approved agency within 180 days of filing. This does not apply for those that are incapacitated, disabled, or on active duty in a military zone.

Some other things to keep in mind:

- Even in bankruptcy if you do not pay the rent, the landlord can evict you.
- All domestic support must be paid in full (child support).
- Monies held in retirement accounts that are tax exempt under the IRS are safe from creditors.
- The so called Chapter 20 bankruptcy is eliminated—time between Chapter 7 filings is now 8 years instead of six. Debtors must also wait two years after receiving a Chapter 13 discharge to refile, or three years if the debtor received a discharge under Chapters 7, 11, or 12.
- Homeowner association fees or condo fees must be paid.

Get a Good Attorney

If you are considering bankruptcy, this is no time to go it alone. You can see how complicated things can get. You need an experienced lawyer who specializes in bankruptcy to navigate the federal laws, state laws and tax consequences. Your future lifestyle hinges on getting the best advice and making the smart choices.

How Does Bankruptcy Affect Your Credit?

Filing for bankruptcy, either chapter, will destroy your credit more than anything else you can do. Even if you only file and do not go through with it, the bankruptcy will be reported on your report. If you do this, not only will the bankruptcy show on the report, but all the accounts will still show as negative.

If you go through with the filing, your report will show the bankruptcy, and the accounts included in the bankruptcy will have special notations, such as "Discharged in Bankruptcy."

Bankruptcies, as well as all the accounts that were part of the bankruptcy, stay on your credit report for up to 10 years. **After one year, you can start to reacquire credit in your own name.** If you use some of our techniques, you might be able to do this even sooner. Find a good mortgage broker and you can even buy a house, days after declaring bankruptcy!

Your credit score will take a massive hit of up to 100 points. Whatever your score is now, it will be 50–100 points lower after bankruptcy. From a lender's point of view, they prefer Chapter 13 to Chapter 7 since it implies that you are willing to repay your debts. But in many cases, an actual person no longer reviews your credit application. Only time and new credit references will improve your score after bankruptcy.

CREDIT SECRET: A bankruptcy will lower your credit score by up to 100 points.

Bankruptcy Tips

The only time you should consider bankruptcy is when you have a house on the line with a lot of equity. If all you have are credit card and unsecured debts, they cannot do anything to you anyway. After a while, they will stop bothering you and seven years later those accounts will be wiped away…much sooner than the 10 years a bankruptcy will stay on your report. Plus, you can negotiate with the creditors and have them remove the negatives from your report. You cannot do this after bankruptcy.

If you have a car, chances are the loan is higher than the value of the car. In this case, bankruptcy is not worth the trouble. Let them take the vehicle back. The money you would have to pay the bankruptcy attorney can go towards another car.

CHAPTER 13

Foreclosure

▶Going into Foreclosure

Foreclosure occurs when you do not pay your mortgage payment and the bank takes back the house. Across the country, thousands of people get foreclosed on every month. Contrary to popular belief, the banks don't like to foreclose either. About the only people who benefit from such action are the foreclosure attorneys, who are hired by the banks to do the legal work.

Going into foreclosure can ruin your credit if it is not ruined already. Your mortgage will probably be the largest amount on your report and your greatest liability. Potential creditors do not like to see foreclosures, since it usually means the individual is having serious financial troubles. People do not like losing their homes if they can help it.

The number of payments you can miss before the bank starts the foreclosure process varies from lender to lender. Most lenders will give you at least a couple of warnings before they take any legal action against you.

Your lender does not want to own your house. Since your lender is not in the business of buying residential real estate, they should be happy to discuss an agreement which will let you keep you in your house. They might rewrite your loan, let you pay only interest for a while, lower your payments or even let you skip a few payments. Taking any of the above options will result in your paying even more interest on your loan, but it is worth it to keep your house. If you make any deal with your lender, make sure to include that no late payments should be reported to the bureaus. Also, be certain to get this agreement in writing.

CREDIT SECRET: Your lender is not in the business of buying residential real estate and does not want to own your house.

If you do nothing, your house will be auctioned off and someone will come by to tell you to get out immediately. Do not let this happen to you.

The other three options you have when you can no longer make your mortgage payments are:

- Selling your house
- Just giving it up
- Bankruptcy

If you sell it, you'll need to sell it for at least the amount you owe the lender. Otherwise, you will be responsible for the balance. Your lender can even stop the sale if it's below the mortgage amount. You should discuss selling your house with a very good realtor.

If you are in serious financial trouble and miss one or two mortgage payments, please start considering selling your house as an option. If you want to sell at top dollar, then you need to have your house on the market for at least a couple months. Do not expect any realtor to sell your house in a week. Even if they do, the potential buyer will need about 30 days to get his loan.

If it is too late for a realtor, consider selling to a private real estate investor. You will find "I Buy Houses" ads in your newspaper everyday. These people can save you from foreclosure, but they are in the business to make money. They will not pay market value, but they can move fast and often can pay all cash.

If you can't sell your house, your second option to avoid foreclosure might be to just give the house back to the lender. This is called "Deed In Lieu of Foreclosure." Doing this will result in your losing any equity that you have built up. To do this, call your lender and tell them you will be giving them the deed to the house in lieu of foreclosure. Again, the lender does not want the house and I have seen some lenders tell homeowners that they need to have the house listed with a realtor for 90 days before they would consider such a proposal. This option, if accepted by your lender, will save your credit from having a foreclosure on it.

Your third option is to declare bankruptcy. Depending on your situation, you could go Chapter 7 or 13. If you want to stay in the house and can realistically begin making the payments, this might be the option for you. If there is no way you can make the payments, you need to sell and move.

If you declare Chapter 13, your mortgage payment will actually **increase.** This is because you will agree to pay all fees, and late charges, and pay them in a short amount of time — usually 5 years. So if you can't make your payments now, you will definitely not be able to make them after bankruptcy. And if you stop making bankruptcy payments, the bank can then re-foreclose your house, and this time there will be nothing you can do to stop them.

Every state has different laws as to how long it takes the lender to foreclose. In Florida, you could conceivably not make a payment for 6 months before they can foreclose on you. In Texas, your house will be auctioned 21 days after the lender files the foreclosure papers with the courthouse.

I have only given you a brief summary of your options. If you are going into foreclosure, you need to know all your rights. I recommend you consult a **real estate attorney** so the lender does not take advantage of you. If you contact any other kind of attorney, they will all tell you to file bankruptcy.

Every ad you see on TV and in the yellow pages from an attorney offering you help you keep your house is from a bankruptcy attorney. These people do not care about you or your situation. You are just a fee to them. As a property investor, I have talked to many homeowners who filed bankruptcy in order to save their house, but lost it anyway because of the way the bankruptcy was set up.

CHAPTER 14

Student Loans

As college costs go higher and higher, the percentage of students taking out student loans is increasing. It is estimated that 50% of all undergraduates and 60% of graduate students have student loans.

Sometimes it is the only way to pay for college. But if they can be avoided, they should. Graduating from college is a great feeling, but the weight of several thousands of dollars in debt is not to be taken lightly.

Getting Student Loans

Getting the loan is the easiest part. Normally, they are given to teenagers entering college. In many cases, credit reports are not even checked. The Federal government guarantees many student loans, so banks are very willing to lend to everybody. As long as you do not have any delinquent student loans recorded against you, there should be no problem in getting more.

Once you are accepted at a college or university and request financial aid, the school will put together a financial aid package to help you pay for school. They will compute how much they can give you and how much you have to pay yourself. This computation is a complex formula and will be explained to you by your Financial Aid Officer.

There are different types of loans available and you should be clear on what the differences are before signing anything. Some are from private lenders, while others come straight from the Federal government. Some are guaranteed by the government; some are not. Most loans are deferred, meaning you do not have to pay then while you are in school. Normally, your payments start 6 months after you leave school or you are no longer enrolled at least half-time (as opposed to a full-time student).

HOT TIP: There are a variety of loans available to college students and you should compare all your options before deciding upon one.

Consolidation

You normally get a different loan every semester. So, if it takes you four years to graduate and you take classes two semesters a year, you will graduate with eight different loans. Thus, after you leave school and your deferment period is over, you begin to get statements to pay on your eight loans. You can either pay each loan separately or you can consolidate them into one loan.

Loan consolidation has several benefits:

- Your payments and interest can be lower.
- You only have to deal with one loan and one bank.
- Your credit report is easier to read since you have fewer accounts.
- You can also extend the amount of time over which to repay the loans, but this means you will pay more in interest over

the long run. Example: If your normal repayment period was ten years, and you consolidate to make it twenty years, the payment will be less. You will be paying a whole lot more interest, however, and the total amount you will have paid will be much higher.

- You can have a fixed interest rate instead of the adjustable rate most loans carry.
- You can further reduce the interest rate by making payments on time.

Most lenders will not accept your application for consolidation unless you have at least $7,500 worth of eligible loans. Here are some more things you need to be aware of:

- You can consolidate only some of your loans instead of all of them if you want to.
- If you have subsidized Stafford loans and you consolidate them with your other loans, you lose the Stafford loan subsidies. If you go back to school, the government will not make the interest payments for you.
- If you are married, you can consolidate both spouses' loans together but you both must agree to be responsible in case of divorce. DO NOT DO THIS!

What happens if you cannot pay?

Close to a million people are currently in default (not paying) on their student loans. In 1990, the percentage of people who defaulted on their loans was an amazing 22.4%. Because of this, the Federal government has passed new laws and is becoming more aggressive in collecting. The Department of Education and the IRS have teamed up to make people pay. If you do not pay, the government can keep your tax returns, garnish your wages and even take you to court.

Even so, there are still several options available to you if you cannot pay your loans. Most options are available if you are not already in default, so please try to keep making the minimum payments every month.

Your main options in dealing with student loans are:

- Consolidation
- Cancellation of loans
- Deferment
- Forbearance

If you meet certain criteria, your loan can be wiped out completely:

- You become totally and permanently disabled.
- The student dies.
- You serve in the U.S. military.
- You are a full-time elementary or secondary schoolteacher in an area that is designated as low income
- You are a full-time teacher of children with disabilities in a public or non-profit elementary or secondary school.
- You are a full-time provider of early intervention services for the disabled.
- You are a full-time teacher of math, science, foreign languages, bilingual education or other fields designated as teacher shortage areas.
- You are a full-time employee of a public or non-profit agency servicing low income, high-risk kids and their families.
- You are a full-time nurse or medical technician.
- You are a full-time law enforcement or corrections officer.
- You are a full-time staff member in a Head Start program.
- You are a Peace Corps or VISTA volunteer.
- Your school closed before you could complete your program of study.

- Your school falsely certified that you were eligible for a student loan.

To apply for cancellation, you can call the Department of Education's Debt Collection Service at 800-621-3115.

If you cannot get a total cancellation, you might qualify for a deferment. In a deferment situation, your lender can let you postpone making payments for a certain amount of time. Your interest is also stopped from accumulating during a deferment.

Alternatively, you can get forbearance. This will also allow your lender to let you stop making payments for some time, but your interest will accrue during the forbearance, making your balance higher. Forbearance is easier to obtain than a deferment, however, because unlike deferments, it is not tied to the kinds of loans you have or to the date you got the loans. Also, you can get forbearance if you are already in default.

To get either a deferment or forbearance you must contact your loan holder.

Student Loans and Your Credit Report

As long as your loans are in the deferment period, meaning you are not required to make payments, your loans are not included in your credit score, even though they are listed on your report. They are treated pretty much as inactive accounts that will have to be paid sometime in the future. On your report, each loan will be listed separately and will be labeled as "Deferred," so anyone reading your report can tell that payments are not required.

HOT TIP: Due to the fact that student loans, like mortgages, are constantly being sold from one company to the next, your student loans might be listed multiple times.

This is a very common practice. In fact, the accounts are even labeled as such. The words "may be duplicate account" are listed on many student loans. So, if you have one loan, three different companies might list it and they might all have balances.

These duplicate loans are no big deal. Every lender that looks at your report knows this occurs. And once you pay them off or consolidate them, they should drop off automatically.

Once you begin to make payments, your loans are treated like any other loans and late payments are counted against you. As far as your credit is concerned, it is best to have as small a monthly payment as possible and to pay them off as soon as possible. Talk to two or three loan consolidators to see if consolidation will be good for you.

If your loans are in default or your payments are late, you will need to start by disputing the duplicate accounts so that multiple negative accounts are not shown. Consolidate if possible to zero out the balances in the old account and close them out. This provides you with a new, never late account and shows that you paid off the others.

CHAPTER 15

Identity Theft

HOT TIP: Even if you have not been a victim of identity theft or fraud, you need to read this chapter. It is loaded with information you need to know.

The revision to the FCRA in 2004 made it easier to report Identity Theft. The credit bureaus have been required to set up a single toll free hotline to call, so people can report identity theft. By calling one number, all three bureaus will be alerted. You can get this number by visiting any of the bureaus' websites.

In the course of a normal day, you may write a check at the grocery store, charge a meal at a restaurant, rent a car, mail your tax returns, call home on your cell phone, order new checks or apply for a credit card. Chances are you don't give these everyday transactions a second thought, but someone else may.

The 1990s introduced a new variety of crooks called identity thieves. Their opportunities are your everyday transactions. Each transaction requires you to share personal information: your bank and credit card account numbers; your income; your Social Security number (SSN); and your name, address and phone numbers. An identity thief retrieves some piece of your personal information and uses it without your knowledge to commit fraud or theft. An all-too-common example is when an identity thief uses your personal information to open a credit card account in your name.

Can you completely prevent identity theft from occurring? Probably not, especially if someone is determined to commit the crime, but you can minimize your risk by managing your personal information wisely, cautiously and with heightened sensitivity.

The U.S. Congress asked the Federal Trade Commission to provide information to consumers about identity theft and to take complaints from those whose identities have been stolen. If you've been a victim of identity theft, you can call the FTC's Identity Theft Hotline toll-free at 1-877-IDTHEFT (438-4338). The FTC puts your information into a secure consumer fraud database and may, in appropriate instances, share it with other law enforcement agencies. This is separate from the credit bureau ID theft hotline. Call both.

How Identity Theft Occurs

Despite your best efforts to manage the flow of your personal information or to keep it to yourself, skilled identity thieves may use a variety of methods—both low and hi-tech—to gain access to your data. Here are some of the ways imposters can get your personal information and take over your identity:

- They steal wallets and purses containing your identification and credit cards.
- They steal your mail, including your bank and credit card statements, pre-approved credit offers, telephone calling cards and tax information.
- They complete a "change of address" form at the post office to have your mail sent to them.

- They go through your trash at home and at work looking for personal information.
- They obtain your credit report by posing as an employer, a landlord or someone else that would have a permissible reason to check your credit.
- They get your business or personal records at home.
- They break into your house to get your personal records.
- They use information you share on the Internet.
- They use their friends or other sources to get your information. By paying an employee of a company, they can get personal information from your mortgage application, employment application or any other application for credit.

Here's how they use your information:

- They call your credit card company and change the mailing address by pretending to be you. They then run up the bill and you won't find out until it's too late.
- They open new credit card accounts using your Social Security number, name, and date of birth, and their address. Some people don't find out about this until months later.
- They open a bank account in your name and write bad checks.
- They buy cars in your name by taking out auto loans.
- They make phony checks for your checking account and use up your money.

Minimize Your Risk

While you probably can't prevent identity theft entirely, you can minimize your risk. By managing your personal information wisely, cautiously and with an awareness of the issue, you can help guard against identity theft.

- Before you reveal any personally identifying information, find out how it will be used and whether it will be shared with others. Ask if you have a choice about the use of your information: Can you choose to have it kept confidential?

- Pay attention to your billing cycles. Follow up with creditors if your bills don't arrive on time. A missing credit card bill could mean an identity thief has taken over your credit card account and changed your billing address to cover his tracks.
- Guard your mail from theft. Deposit outgoing mail in post office collection boxes or at your local post office. Promptly remove mail from your mailbox after it has been delivered.
- Put passwords on your credit card, bank and phone accounts. Avoid using easily available information like your mother's maiden name, your birth date, the last four digits of your Social Security number or your phone number, or a series of consecutive numbers.
- Minimize the identification information and the number of cards you carry to what you'll actually need.
- Do not give out personal information on the phone, through the mail or over the Internet unless you have initiated the contact or know who you're dealing with. Identity thieves may pose as representatives of banks, Internet service providers and even government agencies to get you to reveal your Social Security number, your mother's maiden name, your financial account numbers and other identifying information. Legitimate organizations with which you do business have the information they need and will not ask you for it.
- Keep items with personal information in a safe place. To thwart an identity thief who may pick through your trash to capture your personal information, tear or shred your charge receipts, copies of credit applications, insurance

forms, bank checks and other statements you are discarding, like expired charge cards and credit offers you get in the mail.

- Be cautious about where you leave personal information in your home, especially if you have roommates, employ outside help or are having service work done in your home.
- Find out who has access to your personal information at work and verify that the records are kept in a secure location.
- Give your SSN only when absolutely necessary. Ask to use other types of identifiers when possible.
- Don't carry your SSN card; leave it in a secure place.
- Order a copy of your credit report from each of the three major credit reporting agencies every year. Make sure it is accurate and includes only those activities you've authorized.

A Special Word about Social Security Numbers

Your employer and financial institution will likely need your SSN for wage and tax reporting purposes. Other private businesses may ask you for your SSN to do a credit check, such as when you apply for a car loan. Sometimes, however, they simply want your SSN for general recordkeeping. You don't have to give a business your SSN just because they ask for it. If someone asks for your SSN, ask the following questions:

- Why do you need my SSN? How will my SSN be used?
- What law requires me to give you my SSN?
- What will happen if I don't give you my SSN?

Sometimes a business may not provide you with the service or benefit you're seeking if you don't provide your SSN. Getting answers to these questions will help you decide whether you want to share your SSN with that particular business. Remember though that the decision is yours...CHOOSING TO SHARE YOUR PERSONAL INFORMATION—OR NOT.

What happens to the personal information you provide to companies, marketers and government agencies? They may merely use your information to process your order. They may also use it to create a profile about you and then let you know about products, services or promotions. Or, they may share your information with others. More organizations are offering consumers choices about how their personal information is used. For example, many let you "opt out" of having your information shared with others or from being used for promotional purposes.

You can learn more about the choices you have to protect your personal information from credit bureaus, state Departments of Motor Vehicles and direct marketers.

Credit Bureaus

Pre-Screened Credit Offers

If you receive pre-screened credit card offers in the mail (namely, those based upon your credit data), but don't tear them up after you decide you don't want to accept the offer. Identity thieves may retrieve the offers for their own use without your knowledge.

To opt out of receiving pre-screened credit card offers, call 1-888-5-OPTOUT (1-888-567-8688) or go to *www.optoutprescreen.com*. The three major credit bureaus use the same toll-free number to let consumers choose not to receive pre-screened credit offers.

Marketing Lists

Of the three major credit bureaus, only Experian offers consumers the opportunity to have their names removed from lists that are used for marketing and promotional purposes. To have your name removed from Experian's marketing lists, call 1-800-407-1088.

Departments of Motor Vehicles

Take a look at your driver's license. All the personal information on it—and more—is on file with your state's Department of Motor Vehicles (DMV). A state DMV may distribute your personal information for law enforcement, driver safety, or insurance underwriting purposes, but you may have the right to choose not to have the DMV distribute your personal information for other purposes, including for direct marketing.

Not every DMV distributes personal information for direct marketing or other purposes. You may be able to opt out if your state DMV distributes personal information for these reasons. Contact your state DMV for more information.

Direct Marketers

The Direct Marketing Association's (DMA) Mail, E-mail and Telephone Preference Services allow consumers to opt out of direct mail marketing, e-mail marketing and/or telemarketing solicitations from many national companies. Because your name will not be on their lists, it also means that these companies can't rent or sell your name to other companies.

To remove your name from many national direct mail lists, write:

DMA Mail Preference Service
P.O. Box 9008
Farmingdale, NY 11735-9008

To remove your e-mail address from many national direct e-mail lists, visit *http://www.e-mps.org/*

To avoid unwanted phone calls from many national marketers, send your name, address and telephone number to:

DMA Telephone Preference Service
P.O. Box 9014
Farmingdale, NY 11735-9014
For more information, visit *http://www.the-dma.org/*

If You're A Victim

Sometimes an identity thief can strike even if you've been very careful about keeping your personal information to yourself. If you suspect that your personal information has been hijacked and misappropriated to commit fraud or theft, take action immediately and keep a record of your conversations and correspondence. Exactly which steps you should take to protect yourself depends on your circumstances and how your identity has been misused. However, several basic actions are appropriate in almost every case.

Congress recently enacted the Fair and Accurate Credit Transactions Act of 2003 (FACTA) into law, which will amend the Fair Credit Reporting Act (FCRA). This law has provisions that apply to identity theft.

Your First Steps

First, contact the fraud departments of each of the three major credit bureaus. As of April 2003, if you notify one bureau that you are a victim of identity theft, it will notify the other two. Report that your identifying information is being used by another person to obtain credit fraudulently in your name. Ask that your file be flagged with a fraud alert. Add a victim's statement to your report. ("My ID has been used to apply for credit fraudulently. Contact me at [your phone number] to verify all applications.")

Each credit bureau will mail you a free credit report once your file has been flagged with a fraud alert. Fraud alerts are usually placed for 90–180 days. You will want to extend the time period to seven years. Do so in writing following the directions sent in the credit report you receive. You may cancel fraud alerts at any time. In all communications with the credit bureaus, you will want to refer to the unique number assigned to your credit report and use certified, return receipt mail. Be sure to save all credit reports as part of your fraud documentation.

Ask the credit bureaus for names and phone numbers of credit grantors with whom fraudulent accounts have been opened if this information is not included on the credit report. Ask the credit bureaus in writing to remove inquiries that have been generated due to the fraudulent access. You may also ask the credit bureaus to notify those who have received your credit report in the last six months in order to alert them to the disputed and erroneous information (two years for employers).

Be aware that these measures will not entirely stop new fraudulent accounts from being opened by the imposter. Credit issuers are not required by law to observe fraud alerts. Request a free copy of your credit report every few months so you can monitor for fraud. Under a new California law, victims are able to receive one free report each month for the first 12 months upon request. In other states, you may be charged after the first report. Still it is important to check your credit report about every three months during the active phase of the crime.

Call the FTC's hotline at 877-IDTHEFT. Fill out and file an ID Theft Affidavit.

Contact all creditors immediately with whom your name has been used fraudulently, by phone and in writing. You will see evidence of these accounts on your credit reports. Creditors will likely ask you to fill out fraud affidavits. The Federal Trade Commission

(FTC) provides a uniform affidavit form that most creditors accept. No law requires affidavits to be notarized at your own expense. You may choose to substitute witness signatures for notarization if creditors require verification of your signature.

Ask the credit grantors to furnish you and your investigating law enforcement agency copies of the documentation, such as the application and transaction records, showing the fraudulent transactions.

Under Federal law, victims of identity theft can also legally gain access to records from a business that relate to fraud based on identity theft (applications for credit, sales receipts, copies of checks, and other records). A victim of identity theft must provide a copy of the FTC affidavit (or other affidavit acceptable to the business), government-issued identification, and a copy of a police report. The business must provide copies of these records to the victim within 30 days of the victim's request at no charge. The law also allows a victim of identity theft to "deputize" a law enforcement investigator to get access to these records.

If your existing credit accounts have been used fraudulently, get replacement cards with new account numbers. Ask that old accounts be processed as "account closed at consumer's request" (better than "card lost or stolen" because it can be interpreted as blaming you). Monitor your mail and bills for evidence of new fraudulent activity. Report it immediately to creditor grantors. Add passwords to all accounts. This should not be your mother's maiden name or a word that is easily guessed.

If debt collectors attempt to require you to pay the unpaid bills on fraudulent credit accounts, ask for the name of the company, the name of the person contacting you, phone number, and address. Tell the collector that you are a victim of fraud and are not responsible for the account. Ask the collector for the name and contact information for the referring credit issuer, the amount of the debt, account number, and dates of the charges. Ask if they need you to complete their fraud affidavit form or if you can use the Federal Trade Commission form. Follow up in writing to the debt collector explaining your situation. Ask that they confirm in writing that you do not owe the debt and that the account has been closed.

Report the crime to your local police or sheriff's department. You might also need to report it to police departments where the crime occurred. Give them as much documented evidence as possible. Make sure the police report lists the fraud accounts. Get a copy of the report. Keep the phone number of your investigator handy and give it to creditors and others who require verification of your case. Credit card companies and banks may require you to show the report in order to verify the crime.

If you have had checks stolen or bank accounts set up fraudulently, report it to the appropriate check verification companies. Your bank branch should be able to provide you with a fraud affidavit. Put stop payments on any outstanding checks that you are unsure of. Cancel your checking and savings accounts and obtain new account numbers. Give the bank a secret password for your account (not mother's maiden name). If your own checks are rejected at stores where you shop, contact the check verification company that the merchant uses.

If your ATM or debit card has been stolen or compromised, report it immediately. Contact your bank branch and request a fraud affidavit. Get a new card, account number, and password. Do not use your old password. When creating a password, don't use common numbers like the last four digits of your Social Security number (SSN) or your birth date. Monitor your account statement. You may be liable if fraud is not reported quickly. Be sure to read the debit card contract for liability. Some cards are better protected in cases of fraud than others.

Notify the local Postal Inspector if you suspect an identity thief has filed a change of your address with the post office or has used the mail to commit fraud. (Call the U.S. Post Office to obtain the phone number, (800) 275-8777.) Find out where fraudulent credit cards were sent. Notify the local Postmaster for that address to forward all mail in your name to your own address. You may also need to talk with the mail carrier. (Web: *www.usps.gov/websites/depart/inspect*)

The Secret Service has jurisdiction over financial fraud. But, based on U.S. Attorney guidelines, it usually does not investigate individual cases unless the dollar amount is high or you are one of many victims of a fraud ring. To interest the Secret Service in your case, you may want to ask the fraud department of the credit card companies and/or banks, as well as the police investigator, to notify the Secret Service agent they work with. (Web: *www.treas.gov/usss*)

Contact the Social Security Administration (SSA) to report fraudulent use of your SSN such as welfare or Social Security benefit fraud. They do not handle cases of financial or criminal identity theft. As a last resort, you might try to change your number, although we don't recommend it except for very serious cases. The SSA will only change the number if you fit their fraud victim criteria.

To order a replacement Social Security card, complete the SSA's Application for a Social Security card available at *http://www.socialsecurity.gov/online/ss-5.html*, by calling the SSA at (800) 772-1213, or by visiting your local SSA office (*http://s00dace.ssa.gov/pro/fol/fol-home.html*) to request one. You will need to fill out the form and provide the required documentation at your local SSA office to get a replacement card.

Whether you have a passport or not, write the passport office to alert them to anyone ordering a passport fraudulently.

Provide a password which must be used any time your local, cell, and long distance accounts are changed. If your calling card has been stolen or there are fraudulent charges, cancel it and open a new account.

You may need to change your driver's license number if someone is using yours as ID on bad checks or for other types of fraud. Call the state office of the Department of Motor Vehicles (DMV) to see if another license was issued in your name. Put a fraud alert on your license if your state's DMV provides a fraud alert process. Go to your local DMV to request a new number. Fill out the DMV's complaint form to begin the investigation process. Send supporting documents with the completed form to the nearest DMV investigation office.

If the impostor is apprehended by law enforcement and stands trial, write a victim impact letter to the judge handling the case. Contact the victim-witness assistance program in your area for further information on how to make your voice heard in the legal proceedings.

Sometimes victims of identity theft are wrongfully accused of crimes committed by the imposter. If a civil judgment is entered in your name for your imposter's actions, contact the court where the judgment was entered and report that you are a victim of identity theft. If you are wrongfully arrested or prosecuted for criminal charges, contact the police department and the court in the jurisdiction of the arrest. Also contact the state Department of Justice and the FBI. Ask how to clear your name.

Don't give in. Do not pay any bill or portion of a bill that is a result of fraud. Do not cover any checks that were written or cashed fraudulently. Do not file for bankruptcy. Your credit rating should not be permanently affected. No legal action should be taken against you. If any merchant, financial company or collection agency suggests otherwise, restate your willingness to cooperate, but don't allow yourself to be coerced into paying fraudulent bills. Report such attempts to government regulators immediately.

HOT TIP: Ask to speak with someone in the security or fraud department of each fraudulent creditor.

Your Next Steps

Although there's no question that identity thieves can wreak havoc on your personal finances, there are some things you can do to take control of the situation. For example:

- Stolen mail—If an identity thief has stolen your mail to get new credit cards, bank and credit card statements, pre-screened credit offers or tax information, or if an identity thief has falsified change-of-address forms, that's a crime. Report it to your local postal inspector. Contact your local post office for the phone number of the nearest postal inspection service office or check the Postal Service website at *www.usps.gov/websites/depart/inspect*
- Change of address on credit card accounts—If you discover that an identity thief has changed the billing address on an existing credit card account, close the account. When you open a new account, ask that a password be used before any inquiries or changes can be made on that account. Avoid using easily available information like your mother's maiden name, your birth date, the last four digits of your SSN or your phone number, or a series of consecutive numbers. Avoid the same information and numbers when you create a PIN.
- Bank accounts—If you have reason to believe that an identity thief has tampered with your bank accounts, checks or

ATM card, close the accounts immediately. When you open new accounts, insist on password-only access to minimize the chance that an identity thief can violate the accounts.

In addition, if your checks have been stolen or misused, stop payment. Also contact the major check verification companies to request that they notify retailers using their databases not to accept these checks, or ask your bank to notify the check verification service with which it does business. Three of the check verification companies that accept reports of check fraud directly from consumers are:

Telecheck: 1-800-710-9898
International Check Services: 1-800-631-9656
Equifax: 1-800-437-5120

If your ATM card has been lost, stolen or otherwise compromised, cancel the card as soon as you can and get another with a new PIN.

- Investments—If you believe that an identity thief has tampered with your securities investments or your brokerage account, immediately report it to your broker or account manager and to the Securities and Exchange Commission.
- Phone service—If an identity thief has established new phone service in your name, is making unauthorized calls that seem to come from and are billed to your cellular phone, or is using your calling card and PIN, contact your service provider immediately to cancel the account and/or calling card. Open new accounts and choose new PINs.

If you are having trouble getting fraudulent phone charges removed from your account, contact either your state Public Utility Commission for local service providers or the Federal Communications Commission for long-distance service and cellular providers at *http://www.fcc.gov/cib/ccformpage.html* or 1-888-CALL-FCC.

- Employment—If you believe someone is using your SSN to apply for a job or to work, that's a crime. Report it to the Social Security Administrations' Fraud Hotline at 1-800-269-0271. Also call SSA at 1-800-772-1213 to verify the accuracy of the earnings reported on your SSN and to request a copy of your *Social Security statement.*
- Driver's license—If you suspect that your name or SSN is being used by an identity thief to get a driver's license or a non-driver's ID card, contact your Department of Motor Vehicles. If your state uses your SSN as your driver's license number, ask to substitute another number.
- Bankruptcy—If you believe someone has filed for bankruptcy using your name, write to the U.S. Trustee in the Region where the bankruptcy was filed. A listing of the U.S. Trustee Program's Regions can be found at *www.usdoj.gov/ust*, or look in the Blue Pages of your phone book under U.S. Government—Bankruptcy Administration.

Your letter should describe the situation and provide proof of your identity. The U.S. Trustee, if appropriate, will make a referral to criminal law enforcement authorities if you provide appropriate documentation to substantiate your claim. You may also want to file a complaint with the U.S. Attorney and/or the FBI in the city where the bankruptcy was filed.

Criminal Records/Arrests

In rare instances, an identity thief may create a criminal record under your name. For example, your imposter may give your name when being arrested. If this happens to you, you may need to hire an attorney to help resolve the problem. The procedures for clearing your name vary by jurisdiction.

Should I Apply For A New Social Security Number?

Under certain circumstances, SSA may issue you a new SSN at your request if, after trying to resolve the problems brought on by identity theft, you continue to experience problems. Consider this option carefully. A new SSN may not resolve your identity theft problems and may actually create new problems. For example, a new SSN does not necessarily ensure a new credit record because credit bureaus may combine the credit records from your old SSN with those from your new SSN. Even when the old credit information is not associated with your new SSN, the absence of any credit history under your new SSN may make it more difficult for you to obtain credit. And finally, there's no guarantee that a new SSN won't also be misused by an identity thief.

Where There's Help...

The Federal Trade Commission collects complaints about identity theft from consumers who have been victimized. Although the FTC does not have the authority to bring criminal cases, the Commission can help victims of identity theft by providing information to assist them in resolving the financial and other problems that can result from this crime. The FTC also refers victim complaints to other appropriate government agencies and private organizations for further action.

If you've been a victim of identity theft, file a complaint with the FTC by contacting the FTC's Identity Theft Hotline by telephone: toll-free 1-877-IDTHEFT (438-4338); TDD: 202-326-2502; by mail: Identity Theft Clearinghouse, Federal Trade Commission, 600 Pennsylvania Avenue, NW, Washington, DC 20580; or online: *https://www.ftc.gov/ftc/idtheftform.htm*.

In most instances, a conviction for identity theft carries a maximum penalty of 15 years imprisonment, a fine and forfeiture of any personal property used or intended to be used to commit the crime. The Act also directs the U.S. Sentencing Commission to review and amend the federal sentencing guidelines to provide appropriate penalties for those persons convicted of identity theft.

Schemes to commit identity theft or fraud also may involve violations of other statutes, such as credit card fraud, computer fraud, mail fraud, wire fraud, financial institution fraud or Social Security fraud. Each of these federal offenses is a felony and carries substantial penalties—in some cases, as high as 30 years in prison, fines and criminal forfeiture.

Many states have passed laws related to identity theft; others may be considering such legislation. Where specific identity theft laws do not exist, the practices may be prohibited under other laws. Contact your State Attorney General's office or local consumer protection agency to find out whether your state has laws related to identity theft.

Resolving Credit Problems

Resolving credit problems resulting from identity theft can be time-consuming and frustrating. The good news is there are federal laws that establish procedures for correcting credit report errors and billing errors, and for stopping debt collectors from contacting you about debts you don't owe.

Here is a brief summary of your rights, and what to do to clear up credit problems that result from identity theft.

Credit Cards

The Fair Credit Billing Act establishes procedures for resolving billing errors on your credit card accounts. It also limits your liability for unauthorized credit card charges, in most cases, to $50 per card. The Act's settlement procedures apply to disputes about "billing errors." This includes fraudulent charges on your accounts. To take advantage of the law's consumer protections, you *must*:

- Write to the creditor at the address given for "billing inquiries," not the address for sending your payments. Include your name, address, account number and a description of the billing error, including the amount and date of the error.
- Send your letter so that it reaches the creditor within 60 days after the first bill containing the error was mailed to you. If the address on your account was changed by an identity thief and you never received the bill, your dispute letter still must reach the creditor within 60 days of when the creditor would have mailed the bill. This is why it's so important to keep track of your billing statements and immediately follow up when your bills don't arrive on time.

HOT TIP: You *must* send your complaint letter so that it reaches the creditor within 60 days of the erroneous bill being mailed to you.

Send your letter by certified mail and request a return receipt. This will be your proof of the date the creditor received the letter. Include copies (NOT originals) of sales slips or other documents that support your position. Keep a copy of your dispute letter.

The creditor must acknowledge your complaint in writing within 30 days of receiving it, unless the problem has been resolved. The creditor must resolve the dispute within two billing cycles (but not more than 90 days) after receiving your letter.

Debt Collectors

The Fair Debt Collection Practices Act prohibits debt collectors from using unfair or deceptive practices to collect overdue bills that a creditor has forwarded for collection.

You can prevent a debt collector from contacting you by writing a letter to the collection agency telling them to stop. Once the debt collector receives your letter, the company may not contact you again—with two exceptions: They can tell you there will be no further contact and they can tell you that the debt collector or the creditor intends to take some specific action.

A collector also may not contact you if, within 30 days after you receive the written notice, you send the collection agency a letter stating you do not owe the money. Although such a letter should stop the debt collector's calls, it will not necessarily get rid of the debt itself, which may still turn up on your credit report. In addition, a collector can renew collection activities if you are sent proof of the debt. So, along with your letter stating you don't owe the money, include copies of documents that support your position. If you're a victim of identity theft, including a copy (NOT an original) of the police report you filed may be particularly useful.

HOT TIP: If you're a victim of identity theft, include a copy of the police report with your complaint.

ATM Cards, Debit Cards and Electronic Fund Transfers

The Electronic Fund Transfer Act provides consumer protection for transactions involving an ATM or debit card or other electronic ways of debiting or crediting an account. It also limits your liability for unauthorized electronic fund transfers.

It's important to report lost or stolen ATM and debit cards immediately because the amount you can be held responsible for depends on *how quickly* you report the loss.

- If you report your ATM card lost or stolen within two business days of discovering the loss or theft, your losses are limited to $50.
- If you report your ATM card lost or stolen after the two business days, but within 60 days after a statement showing an unauthorized electronic fund transfer, you can be liable for up to $500 of what a thief withdraws.
- If you wait more than 60 days, you could lose all the money that was taken from your account after the end of the 60 days and before you report your card missing.

The best way to protect yourself in the event of an error or fraudulent transaction is to call the financial institution and follow up in writing—by certified letter, return receipt requested—so you can prove when the institution received your letter. Keep a copy of the letter you send for your records.

After notification about an error on your statement, the institution generally has 10 business days to investigate. The financial institution must tell you the results of its investigation within three business days after completing it and must correct an error within one business day after determining that the error has occurred. If the institution needs more time, it may take up to 45 days to complete the investigation—but only if the money in dispute is returned to your account and you are notified promptly of the credit. At the end of the investigation, if no error has been found, the institution may take the money back provided it sends you a written explanation.

HOT TIP: Visa and MasterCard have voluntarily agreed to limit consumers' liability for unauthorized use of their debit cards, in most instances to $50 per card, no matter how much time has elapsed since the discovery of the loss or theft of the card.

A Special Word About Lost or Stolen Checks

While no federal law limits your losses if someone steals your checks and forges your signature, state laws protect you. Most states hold the bank responsible for losses from a forged check. At the same time, however, most states require you to take reasonable care of your account. For example, you may be held responsible for the forgery if you fail to notify the bank in a timely manner that a check was lost or stolen. Contact your state banking or consumer protection agency for more information.

Resources

1. FEDERAL GOVERNMENT

Federal Trade Commission (FTC)—*http://www.ftc.gov/*

The FTC is the federal clearinghouse for complaints by victims of identity theft. Although the FTC does not have the authority to bring criminal cases, the Commission helps victims of identity theft by providing them with information to help resolve the financial and other problems that can result from identity theft. The FTC also may refer victim complaints to other appropriate government agencies and private organizations for action.

If you've been a victim of identity theft, file a complaint with the FTC by contacting the FTC's Identity Theft Hotline by telephone: toll-free 1-877-IDTHEFT (438-4338); TDD: 202-326-2502; by mail: Identity Theft Clearinghouse, Federal Trade Commission, 600 Pennsylvania Avenue, NW, Washington, DC 20580; or online: *www.consumer.gov/idtheft*

2. BANKING AGENCIES

If you're having trouble getting your financial institution to help you resolve your banking-related identity theft problems, including problems with bank-issued credit cards, contact the agency with the appropriate jurisdiction. If you're not sure which agency has jurisdiction over your institution, call your bank or visit *www.ffiec.gov/nic/default.htm*

Federal Deposit Insurance Corporation (FDIC)— *http://www.fdic.gov/*

The FDIC supervises state-chartered banks that are not members of the Federal Reserve System and insures deposits at banks and savings and loans. Call the FDIC Consumer Call Center at 1-800-934-3342, or write: Federal Deposit Insurance Corporation, Division of Compliance and Consumer Affairs, 550 17th Street, NW, Washington, DC 20429.

Federal Reserve System (Fed)—*http://www.federalreserve.gov/*

The Fed supervises state-chartered banks that are members of the Federal Reserve System. Call: 202-452-3693, or write: Division of Consumer and Community Affairs, Mail Stop 801, Federal Reserve Board, Washington, DC 20551. Alternatively you can contact the Federal Reserve Bank in your area. The 12 Reserve Banks are located in Boston, New York City, Philadelphia, Cleveland, Richmond, Atlanta, Chicago, St. Louis, Minneapolis, Kansas City, Dallas and San Francisco.

National Credit Union Administration (NCUA)— *http://www.ncua.gov/*

The NCUA charters and supervises federal credit unions and insures deposits at federal credit unions and many state credit unions. Call: 703-518-6360, or write: Compliance Officer, National Credit Union Administration, 1775 Duke Street, Alexandria, VA 22314

Office of the Comptroller of the Currency (OCC)— *http://www.occ.treas.gov/*

The OCC charters and supervises national banks. If the word "national" appears in the name of a bank, or the initials "N.A." follow its name, the OCC oversees its operations. Call: 1-800-613-6743 (business days 9:00 a.m. to 4:00 p.m. CST); fax: 713-336-4301; write: Customer Assistance Group, 1301 McKinney Street, Suite 3710, Houston, TX 77010; or e-mail: *Customer.Assistance@occ.treas.gov*

Office of Thrift Supervision (OTS)—*http://www.ots.treas.gov/*

The OTS is the primary regulator of all federal and many state-chartered thrift institutions, which include savings banks and savings and loan institutions. Call: 202-906-6000, or write: Office of Thrift Supervision, 1700 G Street, NW, Washington, DC 20552

Department of Justice (DOJ)—*http://www.usdoj.gov/*

The DOJ and its U.S. Attorneys prosecute federal identity theft cases. Information on identity theft is available at *www.usdoj.gov/criminal/fraud/idtheft.html*

Federal Bureau of Investigation (FBI)—*http://www.fbi.gov/*

The FBI is one of the federal criminal law enforcement agencies that investigates cases of identity theft. Local field offices are listed in the Blue Pages of your telephone directory.

Federal Communications Commission (FCC)—*http://www.fcc.gov/*

The FTC regulates interstate and international communications by radio, television, wire, satellite and cable. The FCC's Consumer Information Bureau is the consumer's one-stop source for information, forms, applications and current issues before the FCC. Call: 1-888-CALL-FCC; TTY: 1-888-TELL-FCC; or write: Federal Communications Commission, Consumer Information Bureau, 445 12th Street, SW, Room 5A863, Washington, DC 20554. You can file complaints via the online complaint form at *www.fcc.gov*. Alternatively, you can e-mail questions to *fccinfo@fcc.gov*.

Internal Revenue Service (IRS)—*www.treas.gov/irs/ci*

The IRS is responsible for administering and enforcing the internal revenue laws. If you believe someone has assumed your identity to file federal income tax returns, or to commit other tax fraud, call toll-free: 1-800-829-0433.

U.S. Secret Service (USSS)—*www.treas.gov/usss*

The U.S. Secret Service is one of the federal law enforcement agencies that investigates financial crimes, which may include identity theft. Although the Secret Service generally investigates cases where the dollar loss is substantial, your information may provide evidence of a larger pattern of fraud requiring their involvement. Local field offices are listed in the Blue Pages of your telephone directory.

Social Security Administration (SSA)—*http://www.ssa.gov/*

SSA may assign you a new SSN at your request if you continue to experience problems, even after trying to resolve the problems resulting from identity theft. SSA field office employees work closely with victims of identity theft and third parties to collect the evidence needed to assign a new SSN in these cases.

SSA Office of the Inspector General (SSA/OIG)

The SSA/OIG is one of the federal law enforcement agencies that investigates cases of identity theft. Allegations that an SSN has been stolen or misused should be directed to the SSA Fraud Hotline. Call: 1-800-269-0271; fax: 410-597-0018; write: SSA Fraud Hotline, P.O. Box 17768, Baltimore, MD 21235; or e-mail: *oig.hotline@ssa.gov*

U.S. Postal Inspection Service (USPIS)—*www.usps.gov/websites/depart/inspect*

The USPIS is one of the federal law enforcement agencies that investigates cases of identity theft. USPIS is the law enforcement arm of the U.S. Postal Service. USPIS has primary jurisdiction in all matters infringing on the integrity of the U.S. mail. You can locate the USPIS district office nearest you by calling your local post office or by checking the list at the website above.

U.S. Securities and Exchange Commission (SEC)— *http://www.sec.gov/*

The SEC's Office of Investor Education and Assistance serves investors who complain to the SEC about investment fraud or the mishandling of their investments by securities professionals. If you've experienced identity theft in connection with a securities transaction, write: SEC, 450 Fifth Street, NW, Washington, DC, 20549-0213. You may also call 202-942-7040 or send an e-mail to help@sec.gov.

U. S. Trustee (UST)—*www.usdoj.gov/ust*

If you believe someone has filed for bankruptcy using your name, write to the U.S. Trustee in the region where the bankruptcy was filed. A list of the U.S. Trustee's Regional Offices is available on the UST website, or check the Blue Pages of your phone book under "U.S. Government Bankruptcy Administration." Your letter should describe the situation and provide proof of your identity. The U.S. Trustee, if appropriate, will make a criminal referral to criminal law enforcement authorities if you provide appropriate documentation to substantiate your claim. You may also want to file a complaint with the U.S. Attorney and/or the FBI in the city where the bankruptcy was filed.

The U.S. Trustee does not provide legal representation, legal advice or referrals to lawyers. That means you may need to hire an attorney to help convince the bankruptcy court that the filing is fraudulent. The U.S. Trustee does not provide consumers with copies of court documents. Those documents are available from the bankruptcy clerk's office for a fee.

3. STATE AND LOCAL GOVERNMENTS

Many states and local governments have passed laws related to identity theft; others may be considering such legislation. Where specific identity theft laws do not exist, the practices may be prohibited under other laws. Contact your State Attorney General's office (for a list of state offices, visit *http://www.naag.org/* or your local consumer protection agency to find out whether your state has laws related to identity theft. Alternatively, visit *www.consumer.gov/idtheft/*

4. CREDIT BUREAUS

Equifax—*http://www.equifax.com/*
To order your report, call: 1-800-685-1111
or write: P.O. Box 740241, Atlanta, GA 30374-0241
To report fraud, call: 1-800-525-6285
and write: P.O. Box 740241, Atlanta, GA 30374-0241

Experian—*http://www.experian.com/*
To order your report, call: 1-888-EXPERIAN (397-3742)
or write: P.O. Box 949, Allen TX 75013-0949
To report fraud, call: 1-888-EXPERIAN (397-3742)
and write: P.O. Box 949, Allen TX 75013-0949

Trans Union—*http://www.tuc.com/*
To order your report, call: 800-916-8800
or write:
760 Sproul Road, P.O. Box 390, Springfield, PA 19064-0390.
To report fraud, call: 1-800-680-7289
and write:
Fraud Victim Assistance Division, P.O. Box 6790, Fullerton, CA 92634

Glossary

Account Condition—Indicates the present state of the account, but does not indicate the payment history of the account that led to the current state (i.e., open, paid, charge off, repossession, settled, foreclosed, etc).

Account Number—Unique number assigned by a creditor to identify your account with them.

Accounts in Good Standing—This section lists credit items that have a positive status and should reflect favorably on your creditworthiness. It includes the creditor's name and address, your account number, the status, type and terms of the account, and additional information as reported by your creditors. Some creditors may not report, so all of your accounts may not be listed.

Adjustment—This is the percentage of the debt that is to be repaid to the credit grantors in a Chapter 13 bankruptcy.

AKA—Also Known As.

Annual Fees—A yearly fee charged by credit grantors for the privilege of using a credit card.

Annual Percentage Rate—The cost of credit at a yearly rate.

Appraisal Fee—The charge for estimating the value of property offered as security.

Applicant—A person applying for credit privileges, employment or some other benefit.

Asset—Anything you own that has value or use.

Association Code—Describes the consumer's relationship to an account.

Authorized User—Person permitted by a credit cardholder to charge goods and services on the cardholder's account. If you wish to have your name permanently removed as an authorized user on an account, you will need to notify the credit grantor.

Automated Teller Machines (ATMs)—Electronic terminals located on bank premises or elsewhere through which customers of financial institutions may make deposits, withdrawals or other transactions as they would through a bank teller.

Balloon Payments—A loan with a balloon payment requires that a single, lump-sum payment be made at the end of the loan.

Bankruptcy—A proceeding in U.S. Federal Court that may legally release a person from repaying debts owed. The law contains several chapters, each of which relate to different methods of relief:

> Chapter 7—Straight Bankruptcy (total liquidation of assets)
> Chapter 11—Business Reorganizations
> Chapter 12—Farm Debt Bankruptcy
> Chapter 13—Wage Earner Repayment Plan.

Bankruptcy Discharged—A court order terminating bankruptcy proceedings on old debts.

Bankruptcy Dismissed—A court order that denied a bankruptcy petition making the debtor still liable for all debts.

Bankruptcy Code—Federal laws governing the conditions and procedures under which persons claiming inability to repay their debts can seek relief.

Billing Error—Any mistake in your monthly statement as defined by the Fair Credit Billing Act.

Budget—A financial plan for saving and spending money.

Business Days—Check with your institution to find out what days it counts as business days under the Truth in Lending and Electronic Fund Transfer Acts.

Capacity—Factor in determining creditworthiness. Capacity is assessed by weighing a borrower's earning ability and the likelihood of continuing income against the amount of debt the borrower carries at the time the application for credit is made.

Chapter 7 Bankruptcy—Chapter of the Bankruptcy Code that provides for court-administered liquidation of the assets of a financially troubled individual or business.

Chapter 11 Bankruptcy—Chapter of the Bankruptcy Code that is usually used for the reorganization of a financially troubled business. Used as an alternative to liquidation under Chapter 7. The U.S. Supreme Court has held that an individual may also use Chapter 11.

Chapter 12 Bankruptcy—Chapter of the Bankruptcy Code adopted to address the financial crisis of the nation's farming community. Cases under this chapter are administered like Chapter 11 cases, but with special protections to meet the special conditions of family farm operations.

Chapter 13 Bankruptcy—Chapter of the Bankruptcy Code in which debtors repay debts according to a plan accepted by the debtor, the creditors and the court. Plan payments usually come from the debtor's future income and are paid to creditors through the court system and the bankruptcy trustee.

Charge Card—A card that requires payment in full upon receipt of the statement.

Charge-Off—Action of transferring accounts deemed as uncollectible to a category such as bad debt or loss. Such accounts will usually continue to be worked by collectors, but are no longer considered part of a company's receivable or profit picture.

Civil Action—Any court action against a consumer to regain money for someone else. Usually, it will be a wage assignment, child support judgment, small claims judgment or a civil judgment.

Claim amount—The amount awarded.

Closed Date—The date the account was closed.

Closed End Lease—A lease in which you are not responsible for the difference if the actual value of the item at the scheduled end of the lease is less that the residual value. You may be responsible for excess wear-and-use charges and for other lease requirements, however.

Collection Account—An account that has been transferred from a routine debt to a collection department of the creditor's firm or to a separate professional debt collecting firm.

Collateral—Property acceptable as security for a loan or other obligation.

Co-maker—A creditworthy co-maker is sometimes required in situations where an applicant's qualifications are marginal. A co-maker is legally responsible to repay the charges in the joint account agreement.

Consumer—Person who uses and/or buys goods and services for family or personal use.

Consumer Credit Counseling Service—A non-profit organization that assists consumers in dealing with their credit problems. Consumer Credit Counseling Service has offices throughout the United States that can be located by calling 1-800-388-CCCS (2227).

Cosigner—Person who pledges in writing, as part of a credit contract, to repay the debt if the borrower fails to do so.

Credit Limit/Line of Credit—In open-end credit, the maximum amount a borrower can draw upon or the maximum amount an account can show as outstanding.

Credit Bureau, Local—A local credit bureau that is contracted with Experian, Equifax, or TransUnion to service consumers in a particular ZIP code area.

Credit—A trust or a promise to pay later for goods or services purchased today.

Credit Card—A rectangular piece of plastic, used instead of cash or checks, authorizing payment for goods and services.

Credit Grantor—Person or business furnishing consumer goods and/or services on credit.

Credit History—Record of how a consumer has paid credit accounts in the past; used as a guide to determine whether the consumer is likely to pay accounts on time in the future.

Credit Insurance—Health, life, accident or dispersion of income insurance designed to pay the outstanding balance of debt.

Credit Items—Information reported by current or past creditors.

Credit Limit—The maximum amount of money that can be charged on a particular credit account.

Credit Repair Companies—Individuals or companies that promise to "clean-up" or "erase" a consumer's bad credit and give him/her a fresh start. Also known as Credit Clinics.

Credit Report—A record or file to a prospective lender or employer on the credit standing of a prospective borrower; used to help determine creditworthiness; confidential report on a consumer's payment habits as reported by their creditors to a consumer credit agency. The agency provides the information to credit grantors who have a permissible purpose under the law to review a consumer's report.

Credit Scoring—Tool used by credit grantors to provide an objective means of determining risks in granting credit. Credit scoring increases efficiency and timely response in the credit granting process. Credit scoring criteria is set by the credit grantor.

Creditworthiness—The ability of a consumer to receive favorable consideration and approval for the use of credit from an establishment to whom they applied.

Date Filed—The date that a public record was awarded.

Date of Status—On the credit report, date the creditor last reported information about this account.

Date Opened—On the credit report, indicates the date an account was opened.

Date Resolved—The completion date of dispute satisfaction of a public record item.

Debit Card—Purchases are deducted directly from the consumer's personal checking account.

Delinquent—Accounts classified into categories according to the time past due. Common classifications are 30, 60, 90 and 120 days past due. Special classifications also include charge-off, repossession, transferred, etc.

Default—Failure to repay a loan or otherwise meet the terms of your credit agreement

Direct Marketing—Names and addresses of consumers are obtained from a credit bureau based on a number of criteria requested by a store or company. The consumer then receives a mailing, generally offering a product or service. Catalogs are the largest users of direct marketing.

Discharge—Granted by the court to release a debtor from most of his debts that were included in a bankruptcy. Any debts not included in the bankruptcy, such as alimony, child support, liability for willful and malicious conduct, and certain student loans cannot be discharged.

Disclosures—Information that must be given to consumers about their financial dealings.

Dismissed—When a consumer files a bankruptcy, the judge may decide to not allow the consumer to continue with the bankruptcy. If the judge rules against the petition, the bankruptcy is known as dismissed.

Disclosure—Giving the consumer the nature and substance of what is in his or her credit report as outlined by the FCRA.

ECOA—Standard abbreviation for Equal Credit Opportunity Act. This is a law passed by Congress which ensures that all consumers will be given an equal chance to receive credit. The ECOA says it is illegal for creditors to discriminate against applicants on the basis of their sex, marital status, race, national origin, age or because they get public assistance income.

Electronic Fund Transfer (EFT) Systems—A variety of systems and technologies for transferring funds electronically rather than by check.

End-user—If a company made an inquiry to a consumer's credit report for someone else, this is the name of the person who originally requested the report.

Equifax—One of the three major credit reporting agencies, headquartered in Atlanta, GA. The other two are Experian and TransUnion.

Experian—One of the three major credit reporting agencies, headquartered in Costa Mesa, CA. The other two are Equifax and TransUnion.

Fair Credit and Charge Card Disclosure Act—Amendments to Truth In Lending Act that require the disclosure of the costs involved in credit card plans that are offered by mail, telephone or applications distributed to the general public.

Fair Credit Billing Act—Federal legislation that provides a specific error resolution procedure to protect credit card customers from making payments on inaccurate billings.

Fair Credit Reporting Act—Federal legislation governing the actions of credit reporting agencies.

Fair Debt Collection Practices Act—Federal legislation prohibiting abusive and unfair debt collection practices.

FICO Score—A credit score developed by Fair Isaac & Co. Credit scoring as a method of determining the likelihood that credit users will pay their bills. Fair, Isaac began its pioneering work with credit scoring in the late 1950s and, since then, scoring has become widely accepted by lenders as a reliable means of credit evaluation. A credit score attempts to condense a borrower's credit history into a single number. Fair, Isaac & Co. and the credit bureaus do not reveal how these scores are computed. The Federal Trade Commission has ruled this to be acceptable.

Finance Charge—Amount of interest. Finance charges are usually included in the monthly payment total.

Fixed Rate—An annual percentage rate that does not change.

Garnishment—Legal process whereby a creditor who has obtained judgment on a debt may obtain full or partial payment by seizure of a portion of the debtor's assets (wages, bank account, etc.).

Generation Identifier—Generation identifiers are Jr., Sr., II, III, I, etc.

Geographical Code—This information is received from the Census Bureau and represents the state, Metropolitan Statistical Area, county, tract and block group of the reported address. This code is similar to a ZIP code.

Grace Period—The period allowed where any finance charges are avoided by paying off the balance in full before the due date.

Guarantor—Person responsible for paying a bill.

High Balance—The highest amount that you have owed on an account to date.

Home Equity Loan—A loan based on the difference of the amount of equity paid on a home and the home's current market value.

Installment Credit—Credit accounts in which the debt is divided into amounts to be paid successively at specified intervals.

Installment Loan—A credit account in which the amount of the payment and the number of payments are predetermined or fixed.

Interest—The cost of borrowing or lending money, usually a percentage of the amount borrowed or loaned.

Investigation—The process a consumer credit reporting agency goes through in order to verify credit report information disputed by a consumer. The credit grantor who supplied the information is contacted and asked to review the information and report back; they will tell the agency that the information is accurate as it appears, or they will give the agency corrected information to update the report.

Investigative Consumer Reports—These are consumer reports that are usually done for background checks, security clearances and other sensitive jobs. An investigative consumer report might contain information obtained from a credit report, but it is more comprehensive than a credit report. It contains subjective material on an individual's character, habits and mode of living, which is obtained through interviews of associates. Experian does not provide investigative consumer reports.

Involuntary Bankruptcy—A petition filed by certain credit grantors to have a debtor judged bankrupt. If the bankruptcy is granted, it is known as an involuntary bankruptcy.

Item-specific Statement—Offers an explanation about a particular trade or public record item on your report, and it appears with that item on the credit report. Only one item-specific statement may be added to an item.

Joint Account—A credit account held by two or more people so that all can use the account and all assume legal responsibility to repay.

Judgment—The official court decision of an action or suit. This public record may be listed on a credit report in matters of money and debts owed.

Judgment Granted—The determination of a court upon matters submitted to it; a final determination of the rights of the parties involved in the lawsuit.

Last Reported—On the credit report, the date the creditor last reported information about the account.

Late Payment—A payment made later than agreed upon in a credit contract and on which additional charges may be imposed.

Lease—A written document containing the conditions under which the possession and use of real and/or personal property are given by the owner to another for a stated period and for a stated consideration.

Lessee—The party to whom the item is leased. In a consumer lease, the lessee is you, the consumer. The lessee is required to make payments and to meet other obligations specified in the lease agreement.

Lessor—The person or organization who regularly leases, offers to lease or arranges for the lease of the item.

Liability Amount—Amount for which you are legally obligated to a creditor.

Lien—Legal document used to create a security interest in another's property. A lien is often given as security for the payment of a debt. A lien can be placed against a consumer for failure to pay the city, county, state or federal government money that is owed. It means that the consumer's property is being used as collateral during repayment of the money that is owed.

Line of Credit—In open-end credit, the maximum amount a borrower can draw upon or the maximum amount an account can show as outstanding.

Location Number—The book and page number on which the item is filed in the court records.

Mortgage—A lien or claim against real property given by the buyer to the lender as security for money borrowed.

> 1st Mortgage—also known as the "primary" mortgage—has priority over the claims of subsequent lenders for the same property.
>
> 2nd Mortgage— also know as the "secondary" mortgage—is a loan secured by mortgage or trust deed, which lien is "junior" to another mortgage or trust.

Mortgage Identification Number (MIN)—Indicates that a loan is registered with Mortgage Electronic Registration Systems Inc., which tracks the ownership of mortgage rights. This number will follow the homeowner throughout the mortgage.

Most Recent Date—The date of the most recent account condition or payment status. This date is also the balance date.

Notice of Results—If your investigation results in information being updated or deleted, you may request that the reporting agency send the corrected information in your credit history to eligible credit grantors and employers who reviewed your information within a specific period of time. If your investigation does not result in a change to your credit history, the results will not be sent.

Obsolescence—A term used to describe how long negative information should stay in a credit file before it's not relevant to the credit granting decision. The FCRA has determined the obsolescence period to be 10 years in the case of bankruptcy and 7 years in all other instances. Unpaid tax liens may remain indefinitely, although Experian removes them after 15 years.

Open-End Credit—A line of credit that may be used repeatedly, including credit cards, overdraft credit accounts and home equity lines.

Opt In—The ability of a consumer who has opted out to have their name re-added to prescreened credit and insurance offer lists, direct marketing lists and individual reference service lists. Consumers may opt in to receive prescreened credit and insurance offer lists by calling 1-888-5OPTOUT (1-888-567-8688).

Opt Out—The ability of the consumer to notify credit reporting agencies, direct marketers and list compilers to remove their name from all future lists. Consumers may opt out of prescreened credit and insurance offer lists by calling 1-888-5OPTOUT (1-888-567-8688).

Original Amount—The original amount owed to a creditor.

Overdraft Checking—A line of credit that allows you to write checks or draw funds with an EFT card for more than your actual balance, with an interest charge on the overdraft.

Payment Status—Reflects the previous history of the account, including any delinquencies or derogatory conditions occurring during the previous seven years (i.e., current account, delinquent 30, current was 60, redeemed repossession, charge-off, now paying, etc.).

Permissible Purposes—There are legally defined permissible purposes for a credit report to be issued to a third party. Permissible purposes include credit transactions, employment purposes, insurance underwriting, government financial responsibility laws, court orders, subpoenas, written instructions of the consumer or legitimate business needs. As defined in section 604 of the Fair Credit Reporting Act, only the named reasons for requesting a credit report are deemed "permissible." Requests not meeting these criteria must be denied.

Personal Line of Credit—The maximum amount one can owe at any time, based on income, debt and credit history.

Personal Information—Includes information associated with your records that has been reported to a company or individual by you, your creditors and other sources. It may include name variations, your driver's license number, Social Security number variations, your date or year of birth, your spouse's name, your employers, your telephone numbers and information about your residence.

Personal Loan—A loan based on a consumer's income, debt and credit history.

Personal Statement—A general explanation about the information on your report that will appear at the beginning of your report.

Petition—If a consumer files a bankruptcy, but a judge has not yet ruled that it can proceed, it is known as bankruptcy petitioned.

Plaintiff—One who initially brings legal action against another (defendant) seeking a court decision.

Point-of-Sale (POS)—A method by which consumers can pay for purchases by having their deposit accounts debited electronically without the use of checks.

Point Scoring—Refers to the assignment of values to a number of characteristics identified as indicators of a person's creditworthiness (e.g., past history) and is based on the same evaluation process used by a credit grantor in the analysis of an applicant's creditworthiness.

Points and Origination Fees—Fees paid to the lender for the loan. One point equals 1% of the loan amount. Points are usually paid in cash at closing. In some cases, the money needed to pay points can be borrowed, but doing so will increase the loan amount and the total costs. An origination fee covers the lender's work in preparing your mortgage loan.

Potentially Negative Items—This section of the credit report lists any potentially negative credit items or public records that may have an effect on your creditworthiness as viewed by creditors. It includes the creditor's name and address, your account number, the status, type and terms of the account, and additional information as reported to an organization by your creditors. It also includes bankruptcy, lien or judgment information obtained directly from the courts.

Principal—The outstanding balance of a loan, exclusive of interest and other charges.

Public Record Data—Included as part of the credit report, this information is limited to tax liens, lawsuits and judgments that relate to the consumer's debt obligations.

Realized Value—(1) The price the lessor or assignee receives for the leased item at disposition, (2) the highest offer for the leased item at disposition, or (3) the fair market value of the leased item at termination. The realized value may be either the wholesale or the retail value as specified in the lease agreement.

Recent Balance—The most recent balance owed on an account as reported by the creditor.

Recent Payment—The most recent amount paid on an account as reported by the creditor.

Released—This means that a lien has been satisfied in full.

Reported Since—On the credit report, the date the creditor started reporting the account.

Repossession—A creditor's taking possession of property pledged as collateral on a loan contract on which a borrower has fallen significantly behind in payments.

Request an Investigation—If you believe that information on your report is inaccurate, the credit bureau will ask the sources of the information to check their records at no cost to you. Incorrect information will be corrected; information that cannot be verified will be deleted. An investigation may take up to 30 days. When it is complete, you will be sent the results.

Request for Your Credit History—When a credit grantor, direct marketer or potential employer makes a request for information from a consumer's credit report, an inquiry is shown on the report. Grantors only see credit inquiries generated by other grantors as a result of an application of some kind, while consumers see all listed inquiries including prescreened and direct marketing offers, as well as employment inquiries. According to the Fair Credit Reporting Act, credit grantors with a permissible purpose may inquire about your credit information prior to your consent. This section also includes the date of the inquiry and how long the inquiry will remain on your report.

Rescission—The cancellation of a contract.

Residual Value—The end-of-term value of the item established at the beginning of the lease and used in calculating your base monthly payment. The residual value is deducted from the adjusted capitalized cost to determine the depreciation and any amortized amounts. It is an estimate that may be determined in part by using residual value guidebooks. The residual value may be higher or lower than the realized value at the scheduled end of the lease.

Responsibility—Indicates who is responsible for an account; can be single, joint, co-signer, etc.

Revolving Account—Credit automatically available, up to a predetermined maximum limit, so long as a customer makes regular payments.

Risk Scoring Models—A numerical determination of a consumer's creditworthiness. Tool used by credit grantors to predict future payment behavior of a consumer.

Satisfied—If the consumer has paid all of the money the court says he owes, it is known as satisfied.

Secured Credit—Loan for which some form of acceptable collateral, such as a house or automobile, has been pledged.

Secured Credit Card—A credit card secured by a savings account that has been established in advance by the borrower. The amount in the account usually determines the limit on the credit card. These accounts present no real risk factor for creditors and are therefore much easier to obtain.

Security—Property pledged to the creditor in case of a default on a loan; see ***collateral***. Real or personal property that a borrower pledges for the term of a loan. Should the borrower fail to repay, the creditor may take ownership of the property by following legally mandated procedures.

Security Alert—Statement that is added once the credit bureau is notified that a consumer may be a victim of fraud. It remains on file for 90 days and requests that a creditor request proof of identification before granting credit in that person's name. Once a security alert has been added, your report is no longer available for online viewing.

Security Alert Message or Victim Statement—Alerts anyone reviewing your information that certain precautions should be taken because you believe that you are a victim of fraud. It will appear at the beginning of your report. Once you add the security alert message or victim statement, your report will no longer be available for online viewing.

Service Charge—A component of some finance charges, such as the fee for triggering an overdraft checking account into use.

Service Credit—Agreements with service providers. You receive goods, such as electricity, and services, such as apartment rental and health club memberships, with the agreement that you will pay for them each month. Your contract may require payments for a specific number of months, even if you stop the service.

Smart Card—An electronic prepaid cash card, usually sold at banks and exchanged at face value.

Source—The business or organization that supplied certain information that appears on the credit report.

Status—On the credit report, this indicates the current status or state of the account.

Terms—This refers to the terms of your agreement with a creditor, such as 60 months, 48 months, etc.

Third-Party Collectors—Collectors who are under contract to collect debts for a credit department or credit company; collection agency.

Tradeline—Entry by a credit grantor to a consumer's file maintained by a credit-reporting agency. A tradeline describes the consumer's account status and activity. Tradeline information includes names of companies where the applicant has accounts, date accounts were opened, credit limits, type of accounts, balances owed and payment profiles.

Transaction Fees—Fees charged for certain use of your credit line—for example, to get a cash advance from an ATM.

TransUnion—One of three major credit-reporting agencies. The other two are Experian and Equifax.

Truth in Lending Act—Title I of the Consumer Protection Act. Requires that most categories of lenders disclose the annual interest rate, the total dollar cost and other terms of loans and credit sales.

Type—This refers to the type of credit agreement made with a creditor; for example, a revolving account or installment loan.

Type of credit (usually revolving or installment)—On the credit report, explains the history of the account that led to the current status.

Unsecured Credit—Credit for which no collateral has been pledged. Loans made under this arrangement are sometimes called signature loans; in other words, a loan is granted based only on the customer's words, through signing an agreement that the loan amount will be paid.

Vacated—Indicates a judgment that was rendered void or set aside.

Variable Rate—An annual percentage rate that may change over time as the prime lending rate varies or according to your contract with the lender.

Verification—Verifying whether data in a credit report is correct or not. Initiated by consumers when they question some information in their file. Credit bureaus will accept authentic documentation from the consumer that will help in the verification.

Victim Statement—A statement that can be added to a consumer's credit report to alert credit grantors that a consumer's identification has been used fraudulently to obtain credit. The statement requests the credit grantor to verbally contact the consumer by telephone before issuing credit. It remains on file for 7 years, unless the consumer requests to have it removed.

Voluntary Bankruptcy—If a consumer files the bankruptcy on his own, it is known as voluntary bankruptcy.

Wage Assignment—A signed agreement by a buyer or borrower, permitting a creditor to collect a certain portion of the debtor's wages from an employer in the event of default.

Withdrawn—This means a decision was made to not pursue a bankruptcy, a lien, etc.

Writ of Replevin—Legal document issued by a court authorizing repossession of security.

About the Author

Ameen Kamadia has been helping people with their credit and finances since 1994. He started out as a manager for a local credit reporting agency. Today, he owns a mortgage company, a property investment company, and a publishing company. By helping others, he has been given the chance to get back even more in return.

He has assisted hundreds of people in fixing, salvaging, and saving their credit. As an industry insider, Ameen has been invited to several seminars and functions put on by the Big 3 Credit Bureaus. Through his mortgage and investment company, he helps people who have had financially forgettable pasts obtain a home of their own.

Via his monthly newsletter and one-on-one counseling, he continues to reach out to the public. For more information, you can visit *www.creditsparkle.com*

Ameen welcomes your comments. He can be reached via e-mail at: *ameen@creditsparkle.com.*

Index

"They laughed at me when I said I was going to become a Mortgage Broker, but when I made $102,624.15 my first year..."

Mortgage Industry Insider Reveals: How To Become A Mortgage Broker or Loan Officer For Less Than $500 and In Less Than One Month In Most States.

So you want to be a mortgage broker?

Or maybe you're not sure yet.

Let's imagine a little.

Imagine a world, where *you are your own master:*

You have the time to *do whatever you wish.*

You have the ability to *live up to your true potential.*

No limits, no barriers. No handicaps or favoritism or discrimination. *Nothing can hold you back.*

You can *be as successful as you wish.* Your income is only limited by your desire.

No menial labor required. You can work whenever you want, wherever you wish. No time clocks to punch or bosses to bother you.

You can have a respectable white-collar universe. Computers, paper, and air-conditioned offices are your domain. High finance is your game.

Your market is virtually unlimited. Everyone wants and needs your product: money.

And they will do what it takes to get it.

But you don't need any money to get started, you have nothing to risk. The money belongs to someone else, and you make money by helping them distribute it.

No formal education is required. ***Just be yourself,*** and through honesty and integrity you can succeed.

This is the world of the mortgage broker. And a world you can join, if you have what it takes to make a decision.

> "Being a mortgage broker gives me the opportunity to live my life as I desire. It was the best career decision I have ever made. I can now do things I only dreamed of when working for someone else—like going to my son's ball games, and taking my wife out to fancy restaurants. I should have done it sooner."
>
> —*RONALD LEON,* **SEATTLE, WA**

The trails are already worn. No new territory here. Thousands of successful brokers have walked this way before. And all you have to do is follow their path. No guesswork. No risk.

This is not a new opportunity. It has been around since there was money. And it will continue to be around as long as man walks the earth. The only question is, will you be a part of it?

What is it you desire out of life?

- **More money?**
- **Financial security?**
- **A good future for your family?**
- **A chance to help others?**
- **Freedom?**

All these can be yours, easily. If thousands of regular, everyday people can do it, so can you. ***Mortgage brokerage is one of the last***

few remaining businesses, in which you are judged by your output, and not who you know, or where you went to school. It doesn't matter if you went to school at all. It might actually be better if you didn't.

Your income is unlimited. You alone determine your success. No external factors can stop you.

If you ever thought you could do great things, this is the opportunity to show what you can really do.

You don't need any money to get started. You don't even need a computer. All you need is the belief that you can succeed, and the desire to do so.

You can provide a much needed service. Imagine how it feels to get a hug from a man and a woman, who just bought their first house—a dream of theirs for years, and one which they know was made possible only because you were there to help them.

That is the life of a mortgage broker. And our company will fill you in on all the details of this life: both the good and the bad.

First let me explain why I am writing this letter:

My company, Kamrock Publishing has a website, it's called *www.mortgagebrokertraining.com*. This is our main site for mortgage professionals. We have several training and marketing resources available at this site.

But what we didn't have was a way to help people get into the mortgage business. And everyday we would get multiple e-mails from people wanting to know how to get a license, where do they start, how do they find a company to work for, etc.

And after a while, we got tired of answering these e-mails, so we put together the only book available that shows people how to get into the business. It's called,

So You Want To Be A Mortgage Broker?

If you have any questions about what to do to become a mortgage broker, or if you want a behind the scenes look at the world of mortgage brokerage this book will be invaluable to you.

In it, we cover all the questions we were asked repeatedly including several that people need to know but did not know to ask.

Some of the questions answered are:

- **What does a broker do?**
- **How does a broker make money?**
- **What is a mortgage broker?**
- **What is a typical day like?**
- **Do I need a license?**
- **How do I get my license?**
- **So why do lenders work with mortgage brokers?**
- **How does a mortgage broker make money?**
- **How much can I earn?**
- **Can I work from home?**
- **So what exactly does a mortgage broker do?**
- **How do I decide what company to work for?**
- **How do I open my own company?**
- **How do I find lenders to work with?**
- **Is my job secure?**
- **Can I do this part time?**
- **How do I get started?**
- **What do I do first?**
- **How long does it take to start?**
- **What do I have to know?**
- **What exactly does the processor do?**
- **What does an underwriter do?**
- **How do I know if I will be a good broker?**
- **What is an appraiser?**
- **Where do I get the credit reports?**
- **What does the title company do?**

- **How do people choose their broker?**
- **What about the competition?**
- **How do I get clients?**
- **What exactly is mortgage banking?**
- **What is continuing education?**
- **What does the future of the industry look like?**
- **How do I motivate myself?**
- **Isn't mortgages a seasonal business?**
- **How do I hide my inexperience?**
- **And many more...**

And top of all that, I even went out into the field and interviewed 16 current mortgage brokers and loan officers to find out what they had trouble with and how they found success. All 16 interviews are also part of the book!

"This book really helped me save hours of running around trying to find answers. Everything I wanted to know was in your book, and because of it I was able to get into the business much sooner that I expected.

—*Rick Sanchez,* Houston, TX

By covering everything you need to know to start, this book will help you get started *FAST!*

- **It even has a complete directory of websites that will tell you exactly what the licensing requirements are in your state.**
- **It gives several DOs and DONTs to help you get started on the right foot.**
- **It has a self-administered test to see if you would make a good broker or not.**
- **It outlines the keys to success in mortgage brokerage.**

"I had been looking for a new job for a while. I was laid off after 13 years. Your book helped me decide and helped me get started quickly. It really made a difference. Becoming a mortgage broker was a great decision."

—*Douglas Robinson,* Springfield

Let this book be your first investment in a better life. And in order to make it affordable to everyone, we set the price at only $29.97. The choice is yours. If you want to improve your life, ORDER NOW.

Sincerely,
Ameen Kamadia

To Order, you can

1. **Order online at *www.mortgagebrokertraining.com/so.html***
2. **Order via phone by calling 713-782-5626.**
3. **Fax in your order form to 713-782-5659**

Make Me A Mortgage Broker Form

Yes, I too want to make money as a mortgage broker and cash in on the real estate boom! I agree to pay $29.97 plus $9 shipping and handling. Texas residents add $2.47 for sales tax please.

Name ____

Address ______________________________________

City ________________________ State ______ Zip __________

Credit card # ____________________ Expiration date ______

Signature ____________________________________